Traits of the Shepherd

Other Works by Al Hill

Our Evil—God's Good
And Other Sermons from Genesis through Joshua

Things That Kings Can't Do
And Other Sermons from Judges through 2ⁿᵈ Kings, and the Wisdom Books

In the Presence of the Lord
And Other Sermons from the Psalms and the Prophets

Walking with Jesus
And Other Sermons from the Gospel of Matthew

God's Purpose for Your Faith
And Other Sermons from Mark, Peter, James and 1ˢᵗ Peter

From Jerusalem to Jericho
And Other Sermons from the Gospel of Luke and the Acts of the Apostles

Making Peace with Your Father
And Other Sermons from Paul's Letters to the Romans and Corinthians

The Empty God
And Other Sermons from the Shorter Letters of Paul

O Come, Let God Adore Us
And Other Sermons for Advent and Christmas

Not Exactly What They Expected
And Other Sermons for Holy Week and Easter

DEAR TRINITY
Letters from a Pastor to His People

Traits of the Shepherd

And Other Sermons from the Gospel of John,
1st John and Revelation

Al Hill

SOMMERTON
HOUSE

Scripture quotations marked "KJV" are from the King James Version of the Bible.

Scripture quotations marked "RSV" are from the Revised Standard Version of the Bible, copyright © 1946, 1952, and 1971 by the National Council of the Churches of Christ in the United States of America. Used by permission. All rights reserved.

Scripture quotations marked "TLB" are taken from The Living Bible copyright © 1971. Used by permission of Tyndale House Publishers, Inc., Carol Stream, Illinois 60188. All rights reserved.

Scripture quotations marked "NIV" are from the Holy Bible, New International Version®, NIV®, copyright © 1973, 1978, 1984, and 2011, by Biblica, Inc.™ Used by permission of Zondervan. All rights reserved worldwide.

Scripture quotations marked "NRSV" are from the New Revised Standard Bible, copyright © 1989 by the National Council of the Churches of Christ in the United States of America. Used by permission. All rights reserved.

Scripture quotations marked "NLT" are taken from the Holy Bible, New Living Translation, copyright © 1996, 2004 and 2015, by Tyndale House Foundation. Used by permission of Tyndale House Publishers, Inc., Carol Stream, Illinois 60188. All rights reserved.

Scripture quotations marked "ESV" are from the ESV® Bible (The Holy Bible, English Standard Version®), copyright © 2001, by Crossway, a publishing ministry of Good News Publishers. Used by permission. All rights reserved.

Scripture quotations marked "CSB" are taken from the Christian Standard Bible®, Copyright © 2017 by Holman Bible Publishers. Used by permission. Christian Standard Bible®, and CSB® are federally registered trademarks of Holman Bible Publishers.

Cover design by the author.
The image of Jesus as the Good Shepherd on the cover is from a stained-glass window created by Louis Comfort Tiffany as part of a 17-window collection installed by Tiffany Studios in 1926 in Baker Memorial United Methodist Church in East Aurora, New York. The image is used with the kind permission of Baker Memorial UMC (www.bakerchurch.org). And special thanks to Baker Memorial's historian, Robb M. Mair, who provided pictures of the window and background information about it.

ISBN: 978-1-948773-19-5 (sc)

Library of Congress Control Number: 2018906503

To learn more about, or to purchase, this or other works by Al Hill,

go to www.sommertonhouse.com

or www.amazon.com/author/alhill.

Dedication

To my Navy chaplain colleagues and friends
who served honorably with me
over three decades
as the spiritual shepherds and shepherdesses
of sea service men and women
and their families—

and to the Religious Program Specialists
who served alongside us
and supported our ministries in so many ways.

Contents

Indices

Preface

What follows are sermons "in the Key of John."

Of the four Gospels, John's is the lone "non-synoptic"—the one "telling" of the story of Jesus that does not march along in step with the other three as they do with each other.

The First Epistle of John picks up the style, language and subject matter of the Fourth Gospel and rings rich in theological reflection and pastoral concern. And though it does not necessarily outshine the other New Testament letters, its author has certainly set it apart from them—and clearly in the "key" of the Gospel by the same name.

The Book of Revelation is indisputably unique as the Bible's conclusion, though passages in the Gospels and other letters will take up the subjects of end times and last things. And the images and concepts in Ezekiel, Daniel and Zechariah are routinely appropriated and reworked in Revelation to place the Christ Event squarely in its cosmic context—and, again, in the unmistakable style of John.

These sermons from Gospel, Epistle and "Apocalypse" draw frequently on stories and perspectives not found elsewhere in the New Testament, which allows for reflection and investigation of ideas not available (either at all, or in the same way) in any other of their biblical "neighbors." Whether Jesus is helping the caterers at the wedding feast at Cana or conducting night classes for

Nicodemus—whether He is gathering His sheep as their Good Shepherd or resisting efforts to kill Him or crown Him prematurely—Jesus comes out of the pages of John's witness as the Living Water, the Bread of Life and the Light of the world Who is always One with the Father. And He intends for His disciples to be one with the Father as well—through Him.

❧❧

All the sermons in this book were written in full before they were preached. They were written—and extensively formatted—so that I could preach them—to a congregation. These sermons were spoken out loud—to a large group of people—gathered in a sanctuary for worship—which means that they were not written to be read by individuals in whatever private setting and location they (you) may have chosen.

For that reason, some sentences may seem to go on forever (though I have divided up more than a few for your benefit). And some sentences won't seem to go on long enough to be classified as "complete." But that's how we talk to each other in real life. And here I put you on notice: You will encounter an inordinate amount of "em-dashes—"separators"—and I hope you can get used to this practice and "hear" the sermons as I intended them to be heard.

I acknowledge and regret that as a reader, you are at the disadvantage of not being able to "hear" the tone and inflection that were applied to words and phrases. You cannot see the facial expressions, body language and physical gestures that accompanied the words in presentation. You will not be aware of all the contextual understandings I shared with the congregations in the various places these sermons were preached.

On the other hand, you will not have to mentally "screen out" the sounds of babies crying or cell phones ringing just as an important idea is being expressed. You can re-read anything that doesn't make sense the first time. You can go back and look at the scripture to clarify an allusion that may seem (and probably is) obscure. You can take up any sermon in the book at any time you want, rather than being stuck with whatever sermon I decided to preach on any given Sunday. And you can stick your book mark in the middle of a sermon and go do something else for a while. All these benefits were not available to the original audience.

࿇

I was taught as a child to capitalize pronouns and other references to the Father, Son and Holy Ghost. Most biblical translations do not do so today, and general literary conventions discourage the practice. Even so, I continue to capitalize (except when quoting copyrighted material). A practical benefit to you of my doing so may be greater clarity when the subject being referred to might otherwise be unclear.

I added the footnotes in the book while preparing the material for publication. I generally did not interrupt the flow of a sermon to identify particular biblical passages as I preached, or give background information about music, media or historical events as I have done here.

In the scripture references at the bottom of the page, a version is identified when phrases, verses or longer passages are quoted *verbatim*. When scripture has been paraphrased, no version is indicated. The same is true for references whose purpose is to provide biblical support for some affirmation or allusion.

The sermon texts and references come from different versions of the Bible. The text used for each sermon reflects the version available to the congregation of the particular chapel or church where the sermon was preached. There is one exception to this practice: One version I used for several years is no longer available for publication. In its place, I have substituted the English Standard Version, the version used in the last church I served.

To assist preachers and others who might want to maneuver more readily around the material, I have provided a group of

xi

indices in the back. All the footnoted scripture references throughout the book are listed in biblical order at the end. A list of Revised Common Lectionary connections is provided, as are an alphabetized list of sermon titles and a list of sermon texts in biblical order. And because sermons from John, 1st John and Revelation appear (or will) in what will eventually be 10 other volumes of my sermons, I have indicated where they may be found in those books.

⇛⇝

I wrote the sermons in this book because I felt called (and led) to do so. I understood that I had a sacred task to speak God's word to God's people under my pastoral charge. I spent a great deal more time grappling with the words and ideas and insights that became these sermons than the people who hear them on Sunday morning did. As a result, I probably "got more out of them" than anybody else. But I'm sure there's something left for you as well.

As most preachers will confirm, the hours we spent in prayer and preparation are not spent alone, but in the presence—and under the direction—of the Holy Spirit. I pray that, as you read and consider, you will sense that you are not alone, either.

⇛⇝

Sermons

From the Gospel of John

1.

Beholding His Glory

John 1:14 NRSV

And the Word became flesh and lived among us, and we have seen his glory, the glory as of a father's only son, full of grace and truth.

৯৽৽৻

On Christmas Day, we gathered for worship and read the first 14 verses of the Gospel of John. We focused particularly on verse 14: *"The Word became flesh and lived among us…"*

On Christmas Day, we celebrated the birth of a Baby and marveled that God would—could—become a Man.

But there is more in this verse 14: *"The Word became flesh and lived among us, and we have seen his glory."* There is Incarnation: *"The Word became flesh."* And there is Epiphany here, too: *"we have seen his glory."*

But you aren't going to understand what John is saying unless you get behind the English words that translate his Greek words that intentionally reflect Hebrew words rooted deep in the Old Testament story of God and His people.

While John is looking at Jesus, he is also looking back to the time of the Exodus, when the children of Israel saw God saving them from slavery in Egypt[1] and leading them through the wilderness to a promised land.[2] When John says that *"the Word"*—the eternal, all-powerful, creative presence of God—*"became flesh and lived among us,"* the word for "lived" actually means "pitched a tent."[3]

It is the same expression God used when He told Moses on Mount Sinai to have the people build Him a tent sanctuary, a tabernacle, *"...that I may 'live' among them."*[4] And when they built that sanctuary—that sacred tent for God—the Bible says, *"the glory of the Lord filled the tabernacle."*[5]

So the word for "living" or "dwelling"—"pitching a tent"—is directly related to the word for "tabernacle," the tent of meeting between God and man. And both of these words are closely related to *shekinah*, the Aramaic word used in ancient Bible translations for the nearness of God's glory.[6] The tabernacle in the wilderness was the specific physical location where God chose to cause His *shekinah* glory to be visible and available to His people. The same would be true when Solomon built a temple in Jerusalem as a permanent replacement for the sacred tent. Again, the Bible says, *"...the glory of the Lord filled the house of the Lord."*[7] It was the place where people saw and experienced God's *shekinah*.

ॐ⊷ॐ

And now, says John, Jesus Himself is the new tabernacle—the new temple[8]—the particular point on earth where the eternal and

---

[1] Exodus 14:30-31.

[2] Exodus 32:13.

[3] Wilhelm Michaelis, "σκηνη, etc.," in *Theological Dictionary of the New Testament, Volume VII*, Gerhard Kittel, G. W. Bromiley, and Gerhard Friedrich, eds., Grand Rapids, MI: Eerdmans, 1964, p. 386.

[4] Exodus 25:8, NRSV.

[5] Exodus 40:34, NRSV.

[6] Dale Moody, "Shekinah," in *The Interpreter's Dictionary of the Bible, Volume 4*, George A. Buttrick, ed., New York, NY: Abingdon Press, 1962, p. 319.

[7] 1 Kings 8:10-11, NRSV.

[8] John 12:6.

infinite God has chosen for His divine *shekinah* glory to be seen by a humanity He loves[9] and is determined to redeem.[10] In Jesus—the Word become flesh—God has pitched His sacred tent among us and shown us His unique glory. In Jesus, all who receive Him and believe in His Name become God's children[11] who see the visible and powerful glory of God.

Jesus is the human Tabernacle—the human temple—where God causes His *shekinah* glory to dwell—to be visible and available to the world.

"Where in the world is God when I need Him?"[12]

There He is, in Jesus.

John went back into history to find the glory of God and show how God *moved* His glory—His love and His mercy and His faithfulness and His power—from tabernacle to temple to Jesus Christ.

But the Apostle Paul will go in the opposite direction.

৵৽৽

Paul says to Christians, "*...your body is the temple of the Holy Spirit... therefore, glorify God in your body.*"[13]

In other words, let the glory of God be visible and available in your very physical existence. The glory of God dwelled in Jesus because He was the Word Who became flesh. Jesus has given the Holy Spirit,[14] Who is the real and powerful presence of God,[15] to every person who believes that Jesus is that Word-made-flesh.

And now that Jesus—crucified and resurrected—has ascended into heaven,[16] the heart and life—the flesh—of the believer is the

---

[9] John 3:16.
[10] Galatians 4:4-5.
[11] John 1:12.
[12] Psalm 139:7-8; Isaiah 55:6.
[13] 1 Corinthians 6:19-20, NRSV.
[14] John 20:22.
[15] Ephesians 2:18.
[16] Hebrews 9:24.

physical tent—the earthly temple—God has chosen to fill with His glory.[17] The *shekinah* glory of God is now visible and available to you because God has placed it—in the Person of the Holy Spirit— in you. That's why Jesus tells His disciples: *"…he who believes in me will also do the works I do; and greater works than these will he do."*[18]

From the tabernacle to the temple to Jesus—and now to you. God dwells in you and in all believers.

Behold His glory.

&~&

---

[17] 1 Corinthians 3:16.
[18] John 14:12, RSV.

2.

The Cana Process

John 2:1-11 RSV

[1] *On the third day there was a marriage at Cana in Galilee, and the mother of Jesus was there;* [2] *Jesus also was invited to the marriage, with his disciples.* [3] *When the wine gave out, the mother of Jesus said to him, "They have no wine."* [4] *And Jesus said to her, "O woman, what have you to do with me? My hour has not yet come."* [5] *His mother said to the servants, "Do whatever he tells you."* [6] *Now six stone jars were standing there, for the Jewish rites of purification, each holding twenty or thirty gallons.* [7] *Jesus said to them, "Fill the jars with water." And they filled them up to the brim.* [8] *He said to them, "Now draw some out, and take it to the steward of the feast." So they took it.* [9] *When the steward of the feast tasted the water now become wine, and did not know where it came from (though the servants who had drawn the water knew), the steward of the feast called the bridegroom* [10] *and said to him, "Every man serves the good wine first; and when men have drunk freely, then the poor wine; but you have kept the good wine until now."* [11] *This, the first of his signs, Jesus did at Cana in Galilee, and manifested his glory; and his disciples believed in him.*

৯৽৹

It is a joy for me to stand before you in this pulpit again today. Leading you in worship on Sunday is the high point of my week.

But it is not my *whole* week.

The chaplains here at Little Creek[19] have pastoral duties from Monday through Saturday as well. And one of the interesting differences between military chaplains and the civilian pastor of a church is that our weekday ministries are generally directed toward people who are seldom part of the Sunday congregation.

Much of that ministry is devoted to counseling—whether in our offices or in workspaces scattered around the base. And much of that counseling is devoted to marriage.

Most marriage counseling, I've found, falls into one of two general categories. There are those who are determined to get married because they love each other so much they cannot stand to be apart. And then there are those who are debating whether to end their marriage because they have come to dislike each other so much they cannot stand to be together.

Counseling this latter group is hard work, and often unsuccessful. It is heart breaking as well when you consider that everyone in this latter group was at one time in the former group. And you might wonder: How did they get from that group to this? How did they go from loving to loathing—from wanting a wedding to demanding a divorce? What was the process?

I've thought a lot about that process over the years, and I have some ideas. But I have decided that that process is less important than one that would keep "Group One" couples from becoming "Group Two-ers"—or that could reclaim for those in the second group the joy they started out with. A process that could do that would be a valuable thing, though many folks in Group Two—and perhaps the world at large—probably think it would take a miracle.

ॐ·ॐ

And I would agree.

---

[19] At the time I was there, it was the Naval Amphibious Base, Little Creek, Virginia, straddling the Norfolk-Virginia Beach city line. At the time of publication, it is the Joint Amphibious Base, Little Creek-Fort Story.

But there just happens to be such a miraculous process. You can make out the main points of it in the second chapter of the Gospel of John, in the story about the marriage feast at Cana. And for that reason, I have taken to calling it "The Cana Process." I would like to share it with you this morning—but let me begin with a digression.

The story begins: *"On the third day, there was a marriage at Cana in Galilee and the mother of Jesus was there."* A simple fact: There was a marriage, and Mary was there.

Sometimes, because you are a friend, or a relative, a neighbor or a co-worker, you are just "there." You see what's going on in a marriage. You hear what they say to each other—and about each other. You get a front row seat for a show that should be a love story but may just as likely turn out to be a circus tightrope act or a knockdown, drag-out fight.

When all goes well in a marriage, it's a joy to be there. But when the going gets rough, you'd probably rather be "anywhere but." What do you do when you're "there" and a marriage needs help? What does "the friend of the marriage" do when a marriage really *needs* a friend? In John, Chapter 2, Mary is "the friend of the marriage," and she provides us a pretty good example.

Because Mary was there, and a friend, she recognized the problem: *"They have no wine."*

Wine is the symbol of joy in the Bible. Now joy in the Bible is not unmitigated pleasure, but the peace and contentment people feel, despite their difficulties and disappointments, when they know their God is in control. That's biblical joy. With wine, people celebrate their joy and enhance it. No wine: no joy. No joy: big problem!

Did Mary know why they had this problem? The Bible doesn't say. But Mary at least knew they had a problem, as any friend would. You don't have to understand the deep-seated causes or intricate psychological details of a problem to know when it's a "low-joy" or "no-joy" marriage.

11

Mary recognized a problem—and took it to Jesus. Not to some of her friends. Not to her preferred partner in the marriage. Not to her diary or Dear Abby or Dr. Phil or some other TV talk show host.

Mary told Jesus about the problem in that marriage. To translate that into our terms: she prayed about it.

"Okay, we should pray about the problems we discover in the marriages around us. But what should we *do*? What should the friend of a marriage do to make the problem better?"

Let me repeat: Mary prayed about it.

Did Mary, the friend of the marriage, know what to do about the problem?

Again, the Bible doesn't say. But you might suspect that if she had, she would have done it herself—if she could. Sometimes, you think you know what to do when you really don't. Sometimes, you know what to do, but you couldn't do it even if you wanted to. Sometimes, you know you don't know what to do.

The friend of a marriage is always right when he or she, like Mary, takes the problem to Jesus, because Jesus knows what we do not. Jesus can do what we cannot. And Jesus guides us when we "know not."

But what if you get the kind of answer Mary got? What if what Jesus says isn't what you want to hear? What if it doesn't make sense?

Mary got an odd answer from Jesus—and yet, she still trusted Him. She believed He could and would handle the problem in that marriage, even when she did not understand everything about His purpose and process. And she encouraged others to be obedient to Him: *"Do whatever he tells you to do,"* she said.

Not bad for a piece of "friendly" advice.

శ్ర•ఆ

As a matter of fact, when it comes to talking to the husband and wife in a joyless marriage, you could do a lot worse as a friend

12

of that marriage than to urge them to take their problem to Jesus and do whatever He tells them to do.

And may I emphasize the word "whatever"? A little bit of obedience is a pretty pathetic thing. Even 99 percent obedience still qualifies as disobedience. But doing "whatever" Jesus says to do is the kind of obedience that gets water changed into wine, which is quite a miracle, though no greater and no less difficult than changing hard and bitter hearts into sweet, sweet spirits.[20]

Mary was "there," a true friend of the marriage. She prayed for them and pointed them to Jesus—and then she let Him go to work. Marriages need friends, especially marriages that are struggling—or worse. But there's only so much friends can do. Mary did her part, but Jesus worked the miracle. Jesus saved the day. So let us look at what Jesus does for this marriage. Let's look at the Cana Process.

❧❦

The good news for this particular marriage is that they started out on the right foot: They invited Jesus to the marriage.

Invitations are a big part of the marriage process. The guest list can include all kinds of people: family and friends, of course—those close to the bride and groom. But the list can get a little crazy sometimes—and swell out of control. The strangest people get invited for the strangest reasons. Perfect strangers get invited, but Jesus may not.

Jesus comes to every marriage, but He does not come *in* unless He is invited. Of all the guests on the list, Jesus is the most important. Some guests will be forgotten quickly. Others will drift away over time. But once invited, Jesus will come to stay, and the wedding gift He gives is the promise of joy—"till death do us part" joy!

---

[20] See Doris Akers, "Sweet, Sweet Spirit," 1962.

The first and most important step in the Cana Process, then, is this: Invite Jesus to—and *into*—the marriage. *"And the second is like unto it"*[21]: Invite His disciples.

Bring the disciples of Christ—the Church—into the marriage. Make your closest friends Christian friends. Worship, study, and pray with them. Center your social life in the ongoing activities of a church, with the people who share your faith and your godly values.

Ask those who know the joy of God's saving grace to help you keep track of the "wine level" in your marriage.

The Cana Process starts with the guest list: Jesus, His disciples, and friends like Mary. It proceeds with a very down-to-earth understanding of the harsh realities of life. The Bible says, very matter-of-factly: *"When the wine ran out…"* *"When,"* not *"if."*

Hard times come. It is the way of our world. Honeymoons end, and the work begins. Marriages are not made in heaven; they are hammered together right here as the determination of some committed couple collides with the never-ending demands of family and career and the culture at large. Do your best, and the wine still runs out. The joy is lost. *"When"*—not *"if"*!

What do you do then? Just like we said earlier: Take stock, be honest, and confess your shortcomings. Tell Jesus: "We have no wine."

"It's not working out the way we planned—or the way we *didn't* plan but just assumed it would, because we were really, really in love."

And what does Jesus say? "Don't worry; I'll fix everything"?

෨෧

Not exactly.

What Jesus says here is hard to translate from the original Greek of the New Testament. It literally says: *"What to me and to*

---

[21] The phrase is from Matthew 22:39, KJV, where Jesus links loving God with loving our neighbor.

you?" It was probably a local figure of speech, a common expression in the native Aramaic Jesus spoke. His meaning is pretty clear, though—and comes across as surprisingly abrupt and confrontational. "Jesus, we have no wine; our marriage is in trouble!" And Jesus replies, "Is that *My* problem?"

"Hello?! Hold the phone—there must be some static on the line. My marriage is in trouble and You ask me if it's Your problem?! You're Jesus, aren't You? Do Your 'thing'! Give me some help here!"

What an odd question for Jesus to ask—in any language. What did He mean? What does it matter? Whose problem is your marriage problem?

Now Jesus is not by nature rude or insensitive to suffering. He is never unintentionally offensive (unless, of course, you're a Pharisee or something). But here He asks a question you would not expect, and we need to figure out why. It may hold the key to understanding the whole Cana Process.

Whose problem is your marriage problem?

His question implies that it *could* be His—or *not* His. His question also implies that someone else decides whether it is His or not. And, finally, the question Jesus asks implies that if it's not His problem, it's not His responsibility to resolve, either.

Let's "unpack" these implications.

‽⇛⌞

A wine-less, joyless marriage is certainly a problem. It is a problem for the man and woman living in it. It's a problem for the family members directly affected by it and any number of friends and co-workers who see, hear, or sense the fallout from it.

But is it Jesus' problem?

You see, Jesus is the Son of God sent from heaven to restore a broken Creation.[22]

---

[22] Romans 8:19-23.

Jesus has come to seek and to save the lost.[23] Jesus is the Redeemer of a sinful humanity.[24] This is a full-time job.

Everything He does is about this. He has no time for odd jobs on the side. He does not "moonlight" as a miscellaneous relationship repairman.

When the wine runs out of a marriage—when the joy is gone, and the love is lost—it is not His responsibility to fix it—*unless it is part of His divinely-assigned redemptive work*. If that marriage is placed within the realm of His redemptive work, then all the power, grace and love He possesses can and will be brought to bear on its problems, because that marriage is then a vital part of God's overall process, the Cana Process.

And so, husbands and wives must decide if their marriage is just about them and what they want and what they can do by themselves, or whether their marriage belongs to God and is to be an instrument in His hand to help restore His fallen world. You can decide the day you get married, or the day you decide to get married, or the day you first discover what marriage is.

On the other hand, you can wait until the wine has run out to decide, when the heated words flare—when the adulterous thoughts simmer or become deeds—when the cold, hard resolve of divorce sets in. The good news is that you can always decide to make your marriage His responsibility—your joy His concern—your problems His to address.

If your marriage is *your* problem, the wine will run out and Jesus will "be about His Father's business."[25] If your marriage is *His* problem, miracles will happen, because your marriage *is* His Father's business. The decision, Jesus says, is yours.

And let us assume, for the moment, that you have decided to make your marriage the Father's business, to give Jesus control and authority over your most intimate and important human

---

23 Luke 19:10.
24 Titus 2:11-14.
25 Luke 2:49, KJV.

16

relationship: "Yes, Jesus, our marriage is Yours to direct and sustain, and our problems are Your problem."

What's the next step in the process?

We talked about honest appraisal and total obedience earlier as the proper characteristics of the friend of the marriage, and they apply to husbands and wives as well. The next step in the Cana Process is action.

When you decide the problem is Jesus', Jesus takes charge of the problem. And Jesus says, *"Fill the jars with water."*

The wine ran out. The joy was gone.

But they still had water.

৯৯০৯

If wine meant "joy," then water meant "life." It was the basic everyday ingredient of life. There was always water for those willing to go to the well and draw it out. Everybody had water. And Jesus says, *"Fill the jars with water."*

At Cana, the jars were like barrels. Each one held 20 to 30 gallons—and there were six of them!

"Fill'em! Fill every one of them up to the top!" Jesus says. "Pour everything you've got into the process. Give Me whatever and everything you've got to work with."

Jesus says, "Give Me every dream and every dollar. Give Me all your time and all your talents. Pour your life into the process where I direct, and then watch what I will do with it."

So what have we got so far?

Total honesty with Jesus.

Total submission to Jesus.

Total obedience to His Word.

And total involvement in His plan.

৯৯০৯

And then the miracles happen.

"Take some out and take it to the feast." You put everything you had in, but what comes out is much, much more. We're talking "total transformation." Your "water" goes in; His "wine" comes out! And that, my friends, really is "something beautiful" to sing about:

> "All I had to offer Him was brokenness and strife,
> but He made something beautiful of my life."[26]

When it was *your* marriage, *your* joy, *your* wine, it ran out. And it was *your* problem.

When it is *His* marriage, and *His* problem, everything you've got belongs to Him and is given to Him, and He transforms everything into joy—joy enough for you and more: joy enough to share, which is the point of this Cana Process.

When your marriage belongs to Jesus, its purpose is more than keeping you and your partner supplied with joy and happiness. Jesus intends to make your marriage an ever-expanding "spiritual joy factory," transforming your trust and obedience into an endless source of joy and celebration—and transformation—for all within your reach. Your marriage becomes a "local distribution site" for God's global and eternal enterprise of redemption and grace.

Take the miraculous wine—the wondrous joy—and share it. And then watch the total amazement it creates: *"Where did this wine come from?"*

"How, after all this time, can you still be so happy with each other?"

"How, after all you've been through—after all you're *still* going through—can you be so joyful?"

"Why does your marriage just seem to get better and better?"

"You've kept the good wine till now when everybody else usually has to settle for whatever's left. It's like a miracle!"

And you can respond: "It is a miracle."

---

[26] Bill Gaither, "Something Beautiful," 1971.

"Our marriage is Jesus' marriage. Our problems are His problem. Our wine is miracle wine. Our joy is 'Jesus joy.'"

What Jesus gives a marriage is better than any human gift. What Jesus gives a marriage lasts long after everything else is gone. It's amazing, really—totally amazing.

෭෨෧

And that's the point of the Cana Process. The miracle that amazes is the sign of the Savior. The Bible says, "*Jesus demonstrated his glory and his disciples believed in him.*"

When you take your marriage through the Cana Process, you experience a miraculous joy. But the *point* of the process is the revelation of a glory that calls us all to faith and redemption. The marriage that belongs to Jesus is a symbol of His saving power, and the miracle of the wine is His promise of the eternal joy to come.

You have seen the miracle.

You have beheld His glory.

Will you believe?

෭෨෧

John 2:1-11 NRSV

¹ On the third day there was a wedding in Cana of Galilee, and the mother of Jesus was there. ² Jesus and his disciples had also been invited to the wedding. ³ When the wine gave out, the mother of Jesus said to him, "They have no wine." ⁴ And Jesus said to her, "Woman, what concern is that to you and to me? My hour has not yet come." ⁵ His mother said to the servants, "Do whatever he tells you." ⁶ Now standing there were six stone water jars for the Jewish rites of purification, each holding twenty or thirty gallons. ⁷ Jesus said to them, "Fill the jars with water." And they filled them up to the brim. ⁸ He said to them, "Now draw some out, and take it to the chief steward." So they took it. ⁹ When the steward tasted the water that had become wine, and did not know where it came from (though the servants who had drawn the water knew), the steward called the bridegroom ¹⁰ and said to him, "Everyone serves the good wine first, and then the inferior wine after the guests have become drunk. But you have kept the good wine until now." ¹¹ Jesus did this, the first of his signs, in Cana of Galilee, and revealed his glory; and his disciples believed in him.

৵৽

3.

Jesus and Marriage

John 2:1-11 NRSV

Today, you can disregard the title for the sermon printed in the bulletin. We come up with the titles long before we come up with the sermons, and sometimes, when we marry them up, they're just not well suited to each other. I hope to make a better match next time.

Some of you may be inclined to disregard the sermon itself today. You may think what you are going to hear doesn't apply to you. Listen anyway, if you would—you may find a way to apply it, after all is said and done.

Some of you will feel like I am rubbing salt in painful wounds—in some cases, fresh wounds. That is the last thing I would intentionally do, and it grieves me to know that I will be doing so today.

But sometimes it is necessary to cause pain in the process of healing.

And there is a gaping wound in our society today that many have mis-diagnosed and mis-treated so severely that it is now infected and festering in a way that will never heal if left untreated. In fact, if we do not deal with it now, with the most powerful medicine available, it will soon prove fatal to our society—as it has already proved devastating to countless couples and families.

It is time to treat the malignancy in marriage.

Marriage has always been susceptible to the symptoms of sickness. Marital discord is as old as Adam and Eve[27] and divorce was an ungodly accommodation even Moses was compelled to make.[28]

And yet, marriage remained the strong cornerstone of every healthy culture throughout history—until forces in our own lifetime began steadily and remorselessly dismantling marriage's very immune system—in ways—and to an extent—previously unknown.

First, marriage was condemned as oppressive, and then deemed irrelevant due to advances in medical science and human sophistication. Then the purpose and place of marriage were turned upside down. The purpose of marriage was reduced to providing personal pleasure, selfishly, and often unrealistically, defined.

The place of marriage as the permanent foundation for family formation and shared life achievement was altered so radically that it serves for many now as but an optional and temporary epilogue to impulsive sexuality (and the inconvenient consequences that ensue).

The latest secular assault on marriage would demolish the very definition of marriage itself. And to that effort, we say, "There are things that man can make legal that he can never make right." When two men or two women go through the motions of a wedding, the result is "an arrangement," not a marriage.

They have declared to God, "Not Your will, but mine, be done."[29] Nonetheless, God's restriction of marriage to the union

---

[27] Genesis 3.
[28] Deuteronomy 24:1-4; Matthew 19:8.
[29] See Luke 22:42.

of a man and a woman is not intended as a punishment of homosexuals, but as a means to preserve and promote humanity.

The traditional treatment for the anti-marriage virus, in all its forms, has always been found in the Word of God, administered effectively by those who proclaimed and adhered to the wisdom of that Word. The Word of God healed those marriages that had gotten sick (if the participants took their divinely-inspired medicine) and vaccinated those who were entering into marriage, shielding them from the severest of the symptoms of sick marriages.

இ-௧

But in our time, the church became passive and stopped promoting and protecting marriage with the powerful resources of God at its disposal. "Surely, Christians are naturally immune from the things that attack and destroy marriages," we thought (or hoped).

The evidence says otherwise.

Surveys suggest the rate of divorce among Christians is not noticeably different from the rate among non-Christians. Marital infidelity is the scourge of far too many congregations. And many marriages that manage to avoid adultery are also devoid of the vibrancy of love and life.

Our children have been seduced by the permissive and perverted promises of the secular perspective of the age. They do not know what marriage is for, and what is only for marriage. And so, we are forced to grieve for them when the world's deception gives way to reality and they reap what they sow after being assured they would not. We are left condoning—after the fact—behavior that should be condemned, because we feel compelled as Christians to help our children cope with consequences too overwhelming for them to confront alone. And so, we are compelled.

But we must also get back into the marriage promotion and protection business.

We must contend with the evil ideas about marriage embraced by the world around us because we know where those ideas come from, ultimately. We know their author. We know their purpose.

We must not be intimidated by the world's ridicule or hostility. We must not be discouraged by the size or the energy or the resources of those arrayed against us. We have work to do, and we have divine guidance and power for doing it.

So let us begin, and begin here, with our own marriages. Today, let us take our lesson from the Gospel of John—from the story we heard earlier: *"There was a wedding...and Jesus had been invited...."*

Two people had gotten married. Their names are unimportant; their guest list is not.

Jesus was invited to their wedding—and He came. Jesus desires to be present with every bride and groom—He wants to be there for every husband and wife.

If invited, Jesus will come into your marriage. There is no invitation Jesus will not accept. On the other hand, He is not the type to crash a party to which He has *not* been invited.

Jesus had been invited to this wedding—and so had His disciples. His disciples came with Him. They were engaged in this celebration of marriage. They saw what Jesus did for the marriage. They became more committed disciples of Jesus because they were there to witness what He was doing for that marriage. And by being there, they blessed that husband and wife, too.

If you are a husband or a wife, invite Jesus into your marriage. As a disciple of Christ, accept the invitation to be involved in the celebration and support of the marriages in the church.

৵৽ঔ

They are having a party—husband, wife, friends and family, Jesus and His disciples—celebrating this marriage, and marriage in general. And the wine gives out. The Bible doesn't say "why." "Why" doesn't matter.

The wine, which symbolizes "joy"—and life itself—is gone. The party is in trouble. In a sense, the marriage is in trouble. Literally, this sort of thing may not be very common. Figuratively—symbolically—it happens all the time.

Why do so many marriages run out of wine—out of joy—out of life? Husbands and wives are trying to supply all the wine—all the joy—all the life—themselves—which they cannot do, no matter how wonderful they are.

Somebody recognized the problem and told Jesus, Who, as we just mentioned, was conveniently there because He had been invited.

Somebody told Jesus they had a problem. We have a term for that. It's called "prayer." If somebody tells Jesus about your problem for you, it's called *"intercessory* prayer." Either way, it's a good thing to do.

And here's a good piece of advice to go with it: *"Do whatever [Jesus] tells you to do."*

Imagine what impact that approach would have on a joyless, empty marriage. Of course, it might be costly—or inconvenient—or humbling—or incredibly hard. It would also be marriage-transforming.

And what does Jesus say?

He's going to turn water into wine and He says, "Give Me all the water you've got. Give Me something to work with. In fact, give Me *everything* to work with. Give Me every inadequate resource you have so that I can turn it into everything you need."

On their own, this husband and wife ran out of wine. Jesus took on the problem and now there's wine everywhere: more wine, and better wine, than you could imagine.

It's a miracle. The marriage is saved—or the celebration—the joy of it, at least.

But it's a low-key miracle, as these things go. Most people don't know why things at the party are so wonderful—they just know they are. But those who are watching closely know—they know they have Jesus to thank.

But don't misunderstand why Jesus did what He did—why He changed the water into wine—and why He will perform miracles in our marriages—in any marriage to which He is invited.

There was a wedding, and Jesus was there when the wine gave out. And Jesus changed water into wine—wonderful wine. We might call it a miracle that saved the day—their wedding day. But the Bible calls it a *sign* that revealed His glory.

Have you ever thought that maybe the traditional wedding ceremony has it wrong—that mutual joy, help and comfort in prosperity and adversity, and procreation and nurture of children are not the purpose of marriage, but merely the beneficial by-products?

Could it be that God's purpose for marriage is simply to provide Jesus a place—an opportunity—to reveal His glory? Could the marriages in this church be a sign of the glory of Jesus—Jesus working in our marriages, performing miracles in them?

What if we who are husbands and wives focused our time and attention and effort on that purpose? What if we evaluated our marriages based on whether we were allowing Jesus to reveal His glory in them? What if the wine of joy and love in our marriages flowed from seeing His glory at work in us rather than from the extent to which we were able to satisfy our personal desires or those of our marital partner?

What if…?

❧

Marriage might start making a comeback. Marriage might recover from the damage the world is determined to do it. Marriage might—well, who knows—turn water into wine—restore true, godly, glorious joy into marriage—and this, according to the Gospel, is only the first miracle Jesus is going to do.

His disciples saw what He did and believed in Him.

Look what He's doing now.

And believe.

಄⊶ఄ

John 2:13-22 NRSV

[13] The Passover of the Jews was near, and Jesus went up to Jerusalem. [14] In the temple he found people selling cattle, sheep, and doves, and the money changers seated at their tables. [15] Making a whip of cords, he drove all of them out of the temple, both the sheep and the cattle. He also poured out the coins of the money changers and overturned their tables. [16] He told those who were selling the doves, "Take these things out of here! Stop making my Father's house a marketplace!" [17] His disciples remembered that it was written, "Zeal for your house will consume me." [18] The Jews then said to him, "What sign can you show us for doing this?" [19] Jesus answered them, "Destroy this temple, and in three days I will raise it up." [20] The Jews then said, "This temple has been under construction for forty-six years, and will you raise it up in three days?" [21] But he was speaking of the temple of his body. [22] After he was raised from the dead, his disciples remembered that he had said this; and they believed the scripture and the word that Jesus had spoken.

৵৽

4.

When Jesus Cleans House

John 2:13-22 NRSV

So what do we have?

Jesus, the country bumpkin from Galilee comes to town for the big festivities and has a fit when He sees what the big-city Jerusalem boys are doing.

Is it "Gentle Jesus, meek and mild"?[30]

Not today. Today, Jesus is the God-appointed Bull in the Temple china shop—He is a holy Terror.

Jesus goes up to Jerusalem—up to the Temple—for Passover. Jesus knows that the Temple is His Father's House, and it just makes Jesus furious to see what they are doing to it—and to the people who are trying to worship God in it but can't. Jesus understands that He has a Son's responsibility to act.

When He does, the Temple authorities are awfully upset that Jesus would upset their system—their process—their racket. They have authorized this farmer's market in the foyer of the Sanctuary. They have given their "okay." The menagerie wouldn't have moved into the Temple precincts—lock, (live)stock and currency exchange, otherwise. The leaders of the Temple have let a lot of

---

[30] See Charles Wesley, "Gentle Jesus, Meek and Mild," 1742.

things get in the way of the point of the Temple: encounter with God. And you know what, God isn't going to put up with it.

...which brings us to Passover. All this takes place at Passover, when Jesus and all His countrymen—all the Jews—are commanded by scripture to remember that God sent a holy, powerful and terrible agent to clear the way for God's people to come to Him without restriction.[31]

The Angel of Death in Egypt that first Passover looks a lot different than the Lord of life at this most recent remembrance of Passover in Jerusalem, but they're both serving God, getting in the way of those who have gotten in the way of those who want to see and know God.

Jesus has a divine authority to act for God, but the authorities in the Temple don't accept His authority. For His part, Jesus doesn't wait for them to approve His credentials. He simply exercises His divine authority—His authority to do God's will—to do the right thing—to do what God commands Him to do.

Do you understand what Jesus is doing?

When Jesus gets done, you won't find a sacrificial *anything* on the premises of the Temple complex, but the path to God will be clear. What Jesus does to the money-changers and the animal sellers will cost them a lot, but His actions hold the possibility for saving them everything. If only they understand. If only they comply.

The people in charge of the Temple have cluttered up the way to God. And their clutter causes everybody there to suffer because it angers God and alienates people from Him—in His own House. The people in charge of the Temple cut themselves off from God, even in the temple of God, and they put obstacles in the way of others—while insisting the obstacles are essential for the proper worship of God. They impede the way to God most for those who,

---

[31] Exodus 12:1-39.

under the best of circumstances, have the hardest time getting to God.

Jesus cleans house in the Jerusalem Temple. But the people in charge there don't learn, and the Temple will be destroyed even before John can get his Gospel on paper. And because Jesus is a bother to them (in large measure because of this particular event), the leaders arrange to destroy Him.[32] But unlike the Temple, which was never rebuilt, God raises Jesus from the dead on the third day,[33] and makes Jesus and His body of believers the new temple in which His Holy Spirit dwells.[34]

☜•❧

Yes, we refer to this sanctuary where we're meeting as "the House of God." But in a deeper sense, you who believe in Jesus as the Christ are the temple of God, the House in which He has chosen to dwell. God has passed over your sins[35] as He passed over your spiritual ancestors in Egypt. He has created a way for you to approach Him in worship and loving service.[36]

But know that God will continually clean His House. He will confront whatever you may put in the way and drive out everything that clutters the temple of your heart—whatever the cost. So do not clutter your heart with things that will impede your access to God. If you find that you have brought something inappropriate into the inner place of your worship, remove it quickly.[37] If you don't, Jesus is liable to do it for you, at great cost and discomfort.[38] Your heart is the House in which God has now chosen to dwell. Make sure it's ready for His presence.

☜•❧

---

[32] Matthew 26:3-4.
[33] Acts 10:36-40.
[34] 1 Corinthians 3:16.
[35] Romans 3:23-25.
[36] Hebrews 7:18-19.
[37] 1 Corinthians 7:1.
[38] 1 Corinthians 3:13-15.

John 2:13-22 ESV

¹³ The Passover of the Jews was at hand, and Jesus went up to Jerusalem. ¹⁴ In the temple he found those who were selling oxen and sheep and pigeons, and the money-changers sitting there. ¹⁵ And making a whip of cords, he drove them all out of the temple, with the sheep and oxen. And he poured out the coins of the money-changers and overturned their tables. ¹⁶ And he told those who sold the pigeons, "Take these things away; do not make my Father's house a house of trade." ¹⁷ His disciples remembered that it was written, "Zeal for your house will consume me."

¹⁸ So the Jews said to him, "What sign do you show us for doing these things?" ¹⁹ Jesus answered them, "Destroy this temple, and in three days I will raise it up." ²⁰ The Jews then said, "It has taken forty-six years to build this temple, and will you raise it up in three days?" ²¹ But he was speaking about the temple of his body. ²² When therefore he was raised from the dead, his disciples remembered that he had said this, and they believed the Scripture and the word that Jesus had spoken.

☙❧

5.

Cleaning Up, Cleaning Out

John 2:13-22 ESV

Did you know that the Temple in Jerusalem in Jesus' day also functioned as the National Bank of Judea? It was a Jewish Fort Knox, where the national treasury was kept.[39] It was the warehouse of all the accumulated wealth of worship when worship was truly "sacrificial."

They say that tens of thousands of sheep would be sacrificed on the Temple grounds during one Passover week,[40] and every one of those poor—and *pure*—little lambs was purchased from the inventory provided by the Temple—purchased by pilgrims with money that made its way from all over the world into the Temple treasury—and out again to stimulate the local economy and the lifestyles of those who were well-connected with the Temple elites.

And all that "bad" foreign money (that had to be exchanged for good Temple money acceptable in worship) was still money

---

[39] See Neill Q. Hamilton, "Temple Cleansing and Temple Bank," in *Journal of Biblical Literature, Vol. 83, No. 4*, December, 1964, pp. 365-372.

[40] Joachim Jeremias, *Jerusalem in the Time of Jesus: An Investigation into Economic and Social Conditions During the New Testament Period*, Philadelphia, PA: Fortress Press, 1969, p. 82. Josephus' assertion in *The Jewish War*, Book 6, Chapter 9, pp. 422-427 that *hundreds* of thousands of sheep were sacrificed during Passover is challenged by Jeremias.

that was good somewhere, especially if you had a lot of it, which the Temple did. And because the Temple had so much money safely tucked away, people who had money of their own wanted their money stashed in the Temple for safe keeping, too. After all, what better security system could you have against robbers than the wrath of Almighty God?

ॐॐ

But even "the fear of God" didn't fend off those who weren't afraid of God—those who were willing to risk divine retribution to get their fingers on a fortune.

When Herod the Great tore down the second Temple and started building his dazzling new one, he made sure there was a connecting passage between it and his fortress next door[41] so that he could make withdrawals from the vaults when he wanted to, without waiting his turn at the teller window. And when he died, and the Romans moved into his fortress, they made sure a lot of the Temple treasury went to all their approved causes—by approving the priests and other people put in charge of the Temple and of the money maintained there.[42]

Banking was big business for the Temple. So you can understand why some very important people would get upset when Jesus showed up and started messing with their well-oiled and well-organized mercantile machinery. Jesus was okay as long as He was just wandering around the countryside in Galilee,[43] turning water into wine[44] and bread into banquets[45] and storms into clear blue

---

[41] See Asher S. Kaufman, "The 'Stoai' of the Temple Abutted on the Staircase of the Tower of Antonia," *Israel Exploration Journal*, Vol. 63, No. 2 (2013), pp. 219-231.
[42] Hamilton, p. 369.
[43] Mark 1:39.
[44] John 2:1-11.
[45] John 6:1-14.

seas.[46] "Go help the sick and the insane all you want, and all will be well."

But now this Jesus has come up to the big city where big people are involved in big business—where *religion* is big business—and He's getting in the way. These are people who won't put up with prophetic gestures and godly protests that gum up the works of what they've got going on. They've got a major temple to run, even if it means "taking out" a troublemaker—which is exactly what they decide to do.[47]

Not that Jesus is surprised. It's exactly what He expected out of these folks; He told His disciples as much on His way there.[48]

෯෴෯

But Jesus has to go to Jerusalem.[49] He has to go to the Temple and clean out their booming business—because there is another, more important, business they're supposed to be involved in. And their banking business—their buying and selling and trading business—is getting in the way of what God let Solomon[50] and Zerubbabel[51]—and even that slimy King Herod[52]—build a temple on that mountain for: a house of prayer.[53]

What did Jesus say as He snapped that flimsy whip around, and slapped the oxen on the backside to get them moving, and sent the money—and the men who changed it—flying? *"Do not make my Father's house a house of trade."*

It's an allusion to what the prophet Zechariah wrote centuries earlier.[54]

---

[46] Mark 4:35-41.
[47] Matthew 26:3-4.
[48] Matthew 16:21.
[49] Luke 13:33.
[50] 1 Chronicles 28:1-6.
[51] Haggai 1:12-14.
[52] John 2:20.
[53] 2 Chronicles 6:18-21.
[54] Zechariah 14:21.

In the other Gospels, Jesus quotes Isaiah, in whose prophecy God says, *"My house shall be...a house of prayer."*[55]

And there you have it: What should have been "a house of prayer," a place prepared and preserved in such a way that anyone—rich or poor, saint or sinner, Jew or Gentile—could come and commune with God—talk with God and hear His answer, free and unfettered—what should have been "a house of prayer" was being run as a house of trade, a place where the "business" of religion was paramount and everything necessary to keep the business booming was "Priority One."

"If you want to pray, pray. We're not going to stop you. But we're really not going to support you, either. And by the way, if you're going to pray, please stay out of the way, unless, that is, you want to exchange your loose change—for a fee—or buy a bull or some birds for a burnt offering. In which case, step right up—the Temple is open for business."

But Jesus won't have it, and here you have the classic confrontation: the unrealized Redeemer of Israel taking on the corrupt hierarchy of a hollow and spiritually bankrupt religious system. To worldly eyes, Jesus looks like some laughable Don Quixote,[56] tilting like a fool at the Temple's towering windmills of power, money and tradition. What can He accomplish?

But by the time the Gospels are written just a few decades later,[57] it will be the great Temple in Jerusalem that lies in ruins[58] and its seemingly powerful rulers who will be no more, while the crazy Carpenter from the countryside they crucified will have been raised from the dead[59] and returned to His rightful place of

---

[55] Luke 19:46; Isaiah 56:7, RSV.

[56] Miguel de Cervantes, *Don Quixote*, 1605.

[57] The scholarly consensus is that the earliest Gospel (Mark) reached its final form between 65 and 70 AD, while the latest (John) was in existence by the end of the First Century.

[58] The Jerusalem temple was captured and burned by the Romans on August 30, 70 AD. See Josephus, *The Jewish War*, Book 6, Chapter 4, c. 75 AD.

[59] Acts 13:30.

authority in heaven,[60] His followers spreading out across the world[61] and creating, by the power of the Holy Spirit of God, houses of prayer everywhere.[62]

God wants His temples to be houses of prayer, not houses of trade. That's why Jesus told His disciples: *"Do not lay up for yourselves treasures on earth, where moth and rust destroy and where thieves break in and steal; but lay up for yourselves treasures in heaven, where neither moth nor rust destroys and where thieves do not break in and steal. For where your treasure is, there your heart will be also."*[63]

He also told them and others, *"Destroy this temple, and in three days I will raise it up."*

Though Jesus was in the Jerusalem Temple when He said it, John writes that Jesus was referring to His own Body, and that certainly made sense after the Resurrection. In fact, after the Resurrection, and the gift to believers of the Holy Spirit,[64] and especially after the destruction of the Temple, Paul wrote to the Ephesians that the local Christian fellowship was the temple of God[65]—and to the Corinthian Christians that their individual bodies were temples of God.[66]

ॐ∙ॐ

So let's change the metaphor.

Though there are business aspects of a church—including our church—the business of our church is not its "business." Yes, we have to plan, pledge and operate a ministry budget each year. Yes, we are planning, pledging funds for and managing the construction of a building. Yes, we select a governing council to consider and conduct business matters for our church.

---

[60] Ephesians 1:20.
[61] Acts 1:8.
[62] Matthew 28:19-20.
[63] Matthew 6:19-21.
[64] Acts 2:1-4.
[65] Ephesians 2:21.
[66] 1 Corinthians 3:16-17; 6:19.

But that's not what God created Trinity for. God created us to be His House of prayer—to be the body into which God comes to commune with His people and hear their hearts' appeal and speak to their deepest desires about life and eternity with love and grace and peace.

And every time we let some business get in the way of prayer—every time we get more concerned with doing things *for* Him (or the church or the world)—even good things—than we are with being *with* Him—we risk Jesus coming and unceremoniously cleaning out our temple and turning things upside down for us.

❧

And if this is true of our church as God's temple, it is also true of us as individuals—individual Christians who are also temples of God.

There is in each of us the "business" of life. Each of us has those things to which we have devoted much of our time and talent and treasure. Some of these things are aspirations for the future, some are challenges of the present, some have now been relegated to the past. None of these things can be allowed to crowd prayer and the spiritual realities of our relationship with God out of their proper place at the center of our lives. If we do, Jesus will come and drive them out of the temple that God has designed to be a house of prayer.

This can come as a big and unpleasant shock if you think all Jesus came to do was clean you *up*: save you from your sin and get you back in God's good graces. You need to understand that just as God sent Jesus to clean you *up*, He also intends for Jesus to clean you *out*, to rid you and your life of everything that prevents you from being the temple that God created you personally to be—to make you more and more like Jesus Himself, Who never let any business of man get in the way of the business of God.

If you're not finding your faith to be the peaceful pleasure you expected it to be, this may be the reason why: You've let some "business" get in the way of what Jesus saved you for. And Jesus is going to crack the whip until the way is clear for God to come and commune with you the way He wants to, because Jesus has made your life—your body—God's house of prayer—God's holy temple—where God can be *to* you and *with* you what He wants to be.

So, what is Jesus working on in your life? What is He turning upside down right now in order to get you right side up with God? What is He weeding out of the garden of your soul so that you can *"grow, unimpeded, in the grace and knowledge of your Lord and Savior*[67]—and in His image?[68] Whatever it is, you'll be better off when every bit of business in your life is brought under His control[69] and into its proper place in relation to God's purpose for you.[70]

Turns out, Jesus wasn't tilting at windmills. He was—and is—tending the temples of God.

ॐ•ॐ

---

[67] 2 Peter 3:18.
[68] Colossians 3:9-10.
[69] 1 Corinthians 15:27-28.
[70] Matthew 6:33.

John 3:1-17 ESV

¹ *Now there was a man of the Pharisees named Nicodemus, a ruler of the Jews.* ² *This man came to Jesus by night and said to him, "Rabbi, we know that you are a teacher come from God, for no one can do these signs that you do unless God is with him."* ³ *Jesus answered him, "Truly, truly, I say to you, unless one is born again he cannot see the kingdom of God."* ⁴ *Nicodemus said to him, "How can a man be born when he is old? Can he enter a second time into his mother's womb and be born?"* ⁵ *Jesus answered, "Truly, truly, I say to you, unless one is born of water and the Spirit, he cannot enter the kingdom of God.* ⁶ *That which is born of the flesh is flesh, and that which is born of the Spirit is spirit.* ⁷ *Do not marvel that I said to you, 'You must be born again.'* ⁸ *The wind blows where it wishes, and you hear its sound, but you do not know where it comes from or where it goes. So it is with everyone who is born of the Spirit."*

⁹ *Nicodemus said to him, "How can these things be?"* ¹⁰ *Jesus answered him, "Are you the teacher of Israel and yet you do not understand these things?* ¹¹ *Truly, truly, I say to you, we speak of what we know, and bear witness to what we have seen, but you do not receive our testimony.* ¹² *If I have told you earthly things and you do not believe, how can you believe if I tell you heavenly things?* ¹³ *No one has ascended into heaven except he who descended from heaven, the Son of Man.* ¹⁴ *And as Moses lifted up the serpent in the wilderness, so must the Son of Man be lifted up,* ¹⁵ *that whoever believes in him may have eternal life.*

¹⁶ *"For God so loved the world, that he gave his only Son, that whoever believes in him should not perish but have eternal life.* ¹⁷ *For God did not send his Son into the world to condemn the world, but in order that the world might be saved through him."*

そ◆ら

6.

Night School

John 3:1-17 ESV

In the months before you called me here to be your pastor, I was an adjunct instructor in American History at Old Dominion University in Norfolk. I taught at night. That was because I also had a day job—with the Navy—supervising chaplains at the Navy's training bases around the country.

The people in my night school class at Old Dominion also had day jobs—for the most part. Some were right out of high school, but most were older—a few almost as old as I was.

They added night school to their already full lives because they wanted different lives—better lives—and they realized that to change their lives in the way they wanted, they would have to come out at night and learn things they did not know.

Night school goes all the way back to the Bible, as you heard from the Gospel reading today. Jesus held class at night—for a fellow named Nicodemus. But night school was an old and honored tradition in Jewish culture—even before Jesus—and it continues so to the present.[71]

---

[71] Rudolf Schnackenburg, *The Gospel According to St. John, Vol. 1, Introduction and Commentary on Chapters 1—4*, Kevin Smyth, trans., New York, NY: Herder and Herder, 1968, p. 366.

Jewish men came together after their work to study the scripture—with rabbis, if they were available—and with each other, if not. Their "classes" could last well into the night.

In this case, the marvel is not that Jesus taught night school, but that someone like Nicodemus would attend His class, or that Nicodemus could even find the "campus." Jesus is in Jerusalem for Passover, with hundreds of thousands of pilgrim-tourists. It's like being in New Orleans for Marti Gras, or Washington for the Fourth of July or Times Square for New Year's Eve.

But this Galilean upstart has just upset the apple cart (and a lot more) in the Temple by throwing out the merchants and money men.[72] He got their attention by messing with their system, and from then on, they kept track of Him. They may not know "where Waldo is" in that mass of humanity, but they have a GPS lock on Jesus, day and night. And so Nicodemus knows where to find Jesus when he wants to go to school.

But Nicodemus was not a name Jesus should have been expecting to see on His class roster. The first thing the Bible tells us about Nicodemus—even before it tells us his name—is that he is a Pharisee.

The Pharisees are religious, to be sure. But they are also legalists. They are obsessed with the law. They use their superior knowledge of the law to take advantage of other people, according to Jesus.[73] And they have come to hate Jesus because He is not impressed with them, He criticizes them for using the law to circumvent justice,[74] and they can't seem to trap Him when thy try to make Him look bad in front of the public.[75]

And Nicodemus is a Pharisee.

But he is more.

---

[72] John 2:13-16.
[73] Matthew 23:1-4.
[74] Luke 11:42.
[75] Matthew 22:15-22.

Nicodemus is a member of the Jewish ruling counsel. The technical title for this group is the "Sanhedrin."[76] They are from the elite of Jewish society, representing important families in and around Jerusalem where they meet. They call the shots for the Jewish people. There are 70 or 72 members, depending on who you talk to, and they span the religious and political spectrum from far right to far left. But somehow, they are able to make common cause when they have to, as when they go after Jesus for stirring up so much trouble. But all that's in the future.

Early in His ministry, after He's made a splash, but before they've put His face on a "Wanted" poster, Jesus looks around one night and sees Nicodemus—religious legalist—elite council member—*Bible* teacher—grabbing a desk in the front of the room and raising his hand to ask a question.

❧•⚬

"Rabbi, we know you are a teacher who has come from God…"
Nicodemus prefaces his question with a little religious flattery to butter up the Teacher.

But he never gets to ask his question. The Teacher cuts him off in midsentence and starts the lesson: "No one can see the kingdom of God unless he is born again."

This is not the rabbit Nicodemus wanted to set loose for Jesus to chase, and now Nick's got to ask some questions just to try and catch up: *"How can a man be born when he is old?"*

A fair question, since the student here is probably older than the Teacher. But the Teacher is ready with the answer: "You were born physically—you came through water—"flesh gives birth to flesh—but the Spirit"—with a capital "S"—"gives birth to spirit"—your spirit. "Let Me illustrate…" and the Teacher does so, simply and brilliantly: "It's like the wind…."

---

[76] See T. A. Burkill, "Sanhedrin," *The Interpreter's Dictionary of the Bible, Vol. 4*, New York, NY: Abingdon Press, 1962, pp. 214-218.

The new student—new to the class—and, apparently, new to the concept—is still stuck on the first question: "How?" But the Teacher is not sympathetic: "Why don't you know this basic stuff? Haven't you been doing your homework? It's all in the assigned readings. What school did you transfer in from?"

Night school is tough, at least for somebody like Nicodemus. You get to a point in your life when you think you've got things figured out. You've attained an impressive level of status, respect and power in your community. You have your theology all organized in a neat, manageable little system, and then, WHAM! You run into a Teacher Who rubs your face in the fact that you have it all wrong—that you've *always* had it wrong.

This close to the end and you've got to do it all over again—not just this lesson, or this class. You've got to go back to the beginning—the very beginning—not just of school, but of life itself. You've got to be born again—born from above—born of the Holy Spirit of God.

❧

Watching Nicodemus in Jesus' class is like watching somebody who thought he was in his final semester, getting ready to graduate, only to have his new faculty advisor tell him he took all the wrong courses and doesn't have any credits.

"O my God! What am I going to do?"

And, fortunately, it is God that Nicodemus is talking to in the person of this Teacher named Jesus. And the answer Jesus gives him is that it isn't what *you* are going to do; it's what God has already done. Jesus tells him: *"God so loved the world that he gave his one and only Son, that whoever believes in him shall not perish but have eternal life."*

"Will that be on the final exam?"

"That *is* the final exam," Professor Jesus replies.

You get this one right and you pass—you graduate—even if everything else was wrong—which it was. You answer, "I believe in Jesus," and you get the perfect score—no matter what you answered on any other questions.

৯৯৩

Notice that you don't hear much from Nicodemus as the class draws to a close. Night school with Jesus sure wasn't what he was expecting. Ol' Nick has got to be an emotional wreck. He comes into class all confident in his big-man-on-campus self-image. But his Pharisaical lock on the Law and his councilman's clout in the community don't get him anywhere with Jesus. Jesus cuts him down to nothing in no time, stripping away every false claim to pride and position, and exposing him as the worthless failure he is in the eyes of God.

And then, with Nicodemus sitting there in front of Jesus with nothing left to hide the truth of his failure and his humiliation, Jesus shows him how to make God's honor roll—how to graduate from "Life U." with flying colors.

First, he learned that he didn't know anything. Now he knows everything he'll ever need to know. Amazing what you can learn when you sit in class under Jesus!

৯৯৩

Why is night school so important? The answer isn't in the verses we read earlier. But listen to what Jesus says as He concludes His class with Nicodemus:

> *"This is the verdict:*
> *Light has come into the world,*
> *but men loved darkness*
> *instead of light*
> *because their deeds were evil.*
> *Everyone who does evil*
> *hates the light,*
> *and will not come into the light*
> *for fear that his deeds will be exposed.*

> *But whoever lives by the truth*
> *comes into the light,*
> *so that it may be seen plainly*
> *that what he has done*
> *has been done through God."*[77]

&-ભ

Nicodemus goes to night school needing a lot of help, but he is coming out of the darkness, into the light. And what he learns through one night with Jesus is enough to light up the rest of his life—and the rest of his eternity. He learns in the night with Jesus, as God's light overcomes his darkness,[78] that he—Nicodemus—can have his night turned into day. Going to night school shows him how he can have a different life—a better life—a life he desperately needs—a life so completely new and unbelievably wonderful it's like being born—all over again.

Well, class, that's your review for the final exam. Everybody should pass. You know the right answer: "I believe in Jesus, the only begotten Son of God."

Everybody who has the right answer *will* pass.

Are you ready?

&-ભ

---

[77] John 3:19-21.
[78] John 1:4-5.

1 Peter 1:17-23 ESV

In the first of Peter's two letters, the apostle writes to Christians as God's new chosen people, dispersed throughout the world and facing the hostility of the worldly people around them. He encourages their commitment to Christian living by reminding them of the price paid for their new life by Christ Himself.

❧

[17] And if you call on him as Father who judges impartially according to each one's deeds, conduct yourselves with fear throughout the time of your exile, [18] knowing that you were ransomed from the futile ways inherited from your forefathers, not with perishable things such as silver or gold, [19] but with the precious blood of Christ, like that of a lamb without blemish or spot. [20] He was foreknown before the foundation of the world but was made manifest in the last times for the sake of you [21] who through him are believers in God, who raised him from the dead and gave him glory, so that your faith and hope are in God.

[22] Having purified your souls by your obedience to the truth for a sincere brotherly love, love one another earnestly from a pure heart, [23] since you have been born again, not of perishable seed but of imperishable, through the living and abiding word of God.

❧

John 3:1-18 ESV

The very familiar John 3:16 passage is actually a concluding summary of what Jesus told the Jewish leader Nicodemus about man's need for a completely new start in life and what God has done to provide it.

֏ֆ

¹ *Now there was a man of the Pharisees named Nicodemus, a ruler of the Jews.* ² *This man came to Jesus by night and said to him, "Rabbi, we know that you are a teacher come from God, for no one can do these signs that you do unless God is with him."* ³ *Jesus answered him, "Truly, truly, I say to you, unless one is born again he cannot see the kingdom of God."* ⁴ *Nicodemus said to him, "How can a man be born when he is old? Can he enter a second time into his mother's womb and be born?"* ⁵ *Jesus answered, "Truly, truly, I say to you, unless one is born of water and the Spirit, he cannot enter the kingdom of God.* ⁶ *That which is born of the flesh is flesh, and that which is born of the Spirit is spirit.* ⁷ *Do not marvel that I said to you, 'You must be born again.'* ⁸ *The wind blows where it wishes, and you hear its sound, but you do not know where it comes from or where it goes. So it is with everyone who is born of the Spirit."*

⁹ *Nicodemus said to him, "How can these things be?"* ¹⁰ *Jesus answered him, "Are you the teacher of Israel and yet you do not understand these things?* ¹¹ *Truly, truly, I say to you, we speak of what we know, and bear witness to what we have seen, but you do not receive our testimony.* ¹² *If I have told you earthly things and you do not believe, how can you believe if I tell you heavenly things?* ¹³ *No one has ascended into heaven except he who descended from heaven, the Son of Man.* ¹⁴ *And as Moses lifted up the serpent in the wilderness, so must the Son of Man be lifted up,* ¹⁵ *that whoever believes in him may have eternal life."*

¹⁶ *"For God so loved the world, that he gave his only Son, that whoever believes in him should not perish but have eternal life.* ¹⁷ *For God did not send his Son into the world to condemn the world, but in order that the world might be saved through him.* ¹⁸ *Whoever believes in him is not condemned, but whoever does not believe is condemned already, because he has not believed in the name of the only Son of God."*

৵৽

7.

Taking a Mulligan on Life

1 Peter 1:17-23; John 3:1-18 ESV

To put it in golf parlance, you just know that as soon as this fellow Nicodemus made his approach shot with Jesus, he probably wanted to "take a mulligan."[79]

It should have been fine.

Nicodemus should have been a master at this sort of thing, with his credentials and experience. Surely, he had practiced and perfected every part of what he was going to do. When he made contact, it should have been right on target, but Jesus interrupted him—in mid-swing, so to speak—and completely demolished his follow-through. Whatever Nicodemus expected when he showed up to "tee up" with Jesus, you just know from the beginning it isn't going to go the way he expects or hopes.

Jesus, it turns out, plays by a different set of rules than the ones Nicodemus is accustomed to—which is going to make things very interesting—and very, very challenging—for Nicodemus.

---

[79] The term refers to the taking of a second shot to replace a bad first shot, without counting the first. The practice (which is against the official rules of golf) seems to go back to the 1930s to an amateur Canadian golfer named David Bernard Mulligan. The term has now expanded in popular parlance to describe free "do-overs" of all kinds.

"Rabbi, we know that you are a teacher who has come from God...." Good form. Good technique. Proper angle.

"Never mind all that; you've got to be born again," declares Jesus flatly.

Now, play *that* one where it lies!

"How can a man be born when he's old?" The frustration and disbelief in his voice sounds like a guy who just triple-bogied the first hole—a circumstance with which some of us are "not *un*familiar."[80]

All the good intentions and high hopes with which he showed up have evaporated. Now, he's just wondering what he can salvage out of the process.

In fact, what Jesus is pointing out to Nicodemus is that (far from being a master player) Nicodemus is just like everyone else playing the course of life. He needs a mulligan, a do-over, a free shot out of the mess his first shot got him into. But he needs a mulligan, not just for one stroke, not just for one stroke per hole, but for every stroke on every hole all the way through the course. Every shot he's taken has gone awry.

ॐॐ

A lot of people who play golf that poorly just stop playing—though not all, apparently, to hear good golfers talk. But you can't stop playing the course of life just because your tee shots keep flying so very wide of the fairway—and your approach shots never approach anything they're supposed to—and your putts put you farther and farther from your goal.

Every morning, you wake up with a tee time on the course of life and you have to get up and play it—hard and frustrating as it is. That's what we all do. That's what everybody in the world does.

---

[80] Golf legend Bobby Jones commented of Jack Nicklaus' performance in winning the 1965 Masters' Tournament: "Nicklaus played a game with which I am not familiar."

And for many, it's a nightmare. It's just too hard. There are too many hazards. There are too many rules that make anything close to "par" impossible—"Nicodemus rules" you might call them—strict rules—the kind that don't allow for mulligans.

So what do you do?

૭᠆ᢙ

Well, some people cheat.

They lie about their score over the course of life. They improve their "lie"—by which I mean their position on the course. They try to ignore, outsmart or get around the course rules.

Others give up.

Since everybody has to come out and play, they show up, but just go through the motions. They don't care what happens when they take their swings. They don't care whether they swing at all. They just plod along around the course until they get to the end. And, as you would expect—as *they* expect—the scores of those who have given up are atrocious.

But here's an interesting thing: *Their* scores are no more atrocious than the scores of those who cheat or lie or bully their way around the course. That's because, on *this* course, the One Who created the course is the One Who keeps score—for everybody.

૭᠆ᢙ

And so Jesus tells Nicodemus—who is sure that his mastery of the rules, and his vast experience abiding by the rules, have made him a superior and impressive player—that his actual score is just as atrocious as everyone else's.

And Nicodemus, for the first time in his life—after a lifetime confidently playing the course of life and assuming his success—is devastated to learn the truth about his game.

You see, in addition to the cheaters and the "give-uppers," there is another group playing the course of life: the self-deceivers.

Nicodemus and those who play the way he does think they're doing all right—certainly better than everybody else. They think the score they're keeping is the official score, and they think that if their score is better than everybody else's—which they are sure it is—they win—which is how it works in golf, of course—but not, it turns out, on the course of life.

So what are we dealing with here?

৯৩৫

Imagine every person in the world playing the course of life (and I use the term "playing" charitably), and everyone ending up in a hazard of some kind or other. And whether sand or water, they're all sinking in the trap their poor play has landed them in. The quality of play on the course of life has left everyone, not just frustrated and defeated, but in genuine danger—which is why Jesus has neither time nor inclination to swap compliments with Nicodemus or anybody else about the quality of their actually disastrous play. Jesus has got a whole human race to get out of the hazards of life before those self-inflicted dangers do them all in.

And what Jesus tells Nicodemus, the Bible records—because it applies to every human being who will ever set foot on the course of life: "You need a mulligan for the whole thing. You need to do life—all of it—over."

And you begin to realize that the "give-uppers" may be the smartest people on the course after all.

How could you do it all over again? And if you could, how could you do it any better than you did it the first time?

You can't take a mulligan for every stroke. You can't really even take *one* mulligan unless whoever you're playing with "gives" it to you. And who's going to give you a mulligan for every stroke you've ever taken? Who's going to let you—enable you—to do your whole life over? And who *could* do that, even if he would?

৯৩৫

Did I mention that the One Who created the course of life, and keeps score for all the players, appointed a Pro for the course? He's a teaching Pro, and a great One. He can teach you everything you need to know about playing this unique and overwhelming course.

And He can play the course Himself—has played the course—like no one else ever came close to playing it, before or since. Every day, He plays beautifully. Every stroke on ever hole is flawless. His every tee shot is straight and deep into the middle of life's fairway. Every approach is perfectly positioned. Every gentle stroke hits pay dirt, whatever the contours on the way to the heart of the life He's aiming to reach.

And Nicodemus met this Pro one night, though he didn't know Who He was. Oh, Nicodemus knew His name was Jesus, and he knew Jesus was a Teacher Who seemed to play the game pretty well.

But, truthfully, Nicodemus didn't have a clue Who he was dealing with. He didn't know that Jesus was the One—the *only* One—Who could give Nicodemus the miraculous mulligan he needed—the mulligan for a new life and a chance to play the course of life again, alongside this divinely-appointed and divinely-powerful life-Pro Who would make Nick's game in life something out of this world.

But he started finding out—and quick!

৵৽

"But it's not possible!" said Nick.

You better hope it is—and believe it is—and bet your life that it is—because if it's not, there are no mulligans on the course of life and you're stuck with the score you shot, which ain't at all pretty.

"But what about the rules?"

There are still rules, but they are the rules of the course Designer and Creator, and He decides how to enforce them, not the players. And He has decided that there *will* be mulligans—there *must* be mulligans—because otherwise, *nobody* can play the course successfully—except the course Pro, of course. But the course's Creator wants more winners than that. He wants everybody to win.[81]

But, again, the Creator determines what it means to win, and the Pro will determine which of the players have met the criteria.[82] And to win on the course of life, you have to play every day with the Pro as your Partner and Teacher,[83] and accept the mulligan for life He offers you[84]—the do-over for all that has gone before without Him.

As Jesus told Nicodemus:

"…for the Course of Life Creator
so loved all the players
that He sent His only begotten Son
(to the course to be the Pro),
that whosoever believes
that He is the Pro
(Who could and would give them
this miraculous essential
mulligan for life
and would partner with them
to play the course each day)
would not lose,
but win the greatest grand prize
ever awarded on any course,
anywhere, anytime—
for all time…"

…or words to that effect.

৵৽৶

---

81 2 Peter 3:9.
82 John 5:22.
83 Luke 9:23.
84 Romans 6:23.

8.

The Motive for the Messiah

John 3:14-21 NRSV

[Jesus said:]

¹⁴ "And just as Moses lifted up the serpent in the wilderness, so must the Son of Man be lifted up, ¹⁵ that whoever believes in him may have eternal life.

¹⁶ "For God so loved the world that he gave his only Son, so that everyone who believes in him may not perish but may have eternal life.

¹⁷ "Indeed, God did not send the Son into the world to condemn the world, but in order that the world might be saved through him. ¹⁸ Those who believe in him are not condemned; but those who do not believe are condemned already, because they have not believed in the name of the only Son of God. ¹⁹ And this is the judgment, that the light has come into the world, and people loved darkness rather than light because their deeds were evil. ²⁰ For all who do evil hate the light and do not come to the light, so that their deeds may not be exposed. ²¹ But those who do what is true come to the light, so that it may be clearly seen that their deeds have been done in God."

కావ

John 3:16. Perhaps the most familiar verse in the Bible. Martin Luther called it "the gospel in miniature." If you memorized verses as a child, this would have been one of the first. You may still be able to recite it. You will probably see it on TV today (or, at least the reference) if you watch a ball game later on. Somebody will hold up a poster in the crowd, or the camera will catch a close up of it painted on someone's face. John 3:16—everybody knows that verse.

You know the words, certainly. But do you know the meaning of the words? Do you know the message conveyed in these almost *too* familiar words?

Luther was right: It is the gospel in miniature. Its 25 words or so suggest far more than they say, even though they say quite a lot. The familiar words point all over the Bible, and following the clues will reveal a picture that is far bigger, broader, and bolder than you may imagine.

☙❧

The first clue is the first word: "for." *"For God so loved the world..."* "For" means "because." John 3:16 is the reason for something. That "something" is found close by, in the verses just before, where Jesus says, *"the Son of man [must] be lifted up."* To say He "must be" means that it is necessary, essential, mandatory. It is what God has decided, and so it will happen. He *will* be lifted up— He *must* be lifted up—*because—for—"God so loved the world."*

Because God so loved the world, the Son of man must be lifted up. But what does it mean for the Son of man to be "lifted up"?

It means the same thing as Moses lifting up the serpent in the wilderness, which takes us to the 21st Chapter of Numbers in the Old Testament, 1,200 years before Jesus. It reads, *"The people spoke against God and against Moses…. The LORD sent fiery serpents among the people, and they bit the people, so that many of the people of Israel died."*[85]

Those that weren't dead yet had a sudden change of attitude, which is not uncommon in such circumstances, and asked Moses to pray the snakes away. Moses prayed, and God had him lift up a

---

[85] Numbers 21:5-6, RSV.

bronze snake on a pole that people could look at and survive as a result.

They still got bitten—they had "earned" their serpents—but God provided them a salvation amid the snakes—a salvation they had to have but didn't deserve. God provided a lifted-up symbol of salvation *because—for*—God so loved the children of Israel.

❧

And now, some 12 centuries later, Jesus says God is doing the same thing because God loves the whole world in the same way He loved His chosen people in the Wilderness "way back when." God is doing the same thing in the same way—that's what the little word "so" means: *"as Moses lifted up the serpent...* ***so*** *must the Son of man be lifted up"*—in the same way.

Why "in the same way"?

So that those who know what happened in the Wilderness—who know that the symbol of God's salvation was lifted up for dying people to see and be saved by—will recognize that God is doing it again. He's lifting up the Son of man in the same way—for the same purpose.

"For God so loved the world..." "For" means "because." "So" means "in the same way." And what does "loved" mean?

Here's a hint: John 3:16 is not talking about how God *felt.*

In the original language, there were ways to say things were in a continuous, on-going state, and ways to say that something was a one-time event, now completed. John 3:16 says that God loved the world in a one-time event now completed.

Does this mean that God doesn't love the world anymore? Is He "over" us?

Thank God, no! God continues to feel as He has always felt.

So what does it mean?

❧

Paul may be able to help us here with the meaning of John 3:16. Paul says in Romans, Chapter 5, that *"God showed his love for us in that while we were yet sinners, Christ died for us."*[86] God loved us once, in a very unique action that has been completed.

God expressed His love—demonstrated His love—loved in action, not merely in sentiment—and did so, so profoundly and effectively—that that particular act of love would never have to be performed again.

What was that ultimate, unrepeatable act of love? How did God bestow love upon the world?

John 3:16 says, *"...he gave his only Son..."*

That's what it says. But what does it mean?

The clue for that is in the words "gave" and "only." These are special words with special meanings. The first—"gave"—means "gave as an offering"—"gave to be sacrificed."

It also means, "gave freely and voluntarily" because, of course, nothing taken, forced, or coerced is an offering. Paul catches the meaning when he writes in Ephesians, *"Christ loved us and gave himself up for us, as a fragrant offering and sacrifice to God."*[87]

Like Father—like Son. God demonstrated His love by giving His Son to be a sacrifice.

He gave His *only* (or, if you remember the King James Version better, *only begotten*) Son. But the Greek word, whichever way it is translated, is really more about uniqueness—being unlike any other—the only one of its (or His) kind. It is the same word used in Hebrews 11, where it says *"Abraham, when he was tested, offered up Isaac...his **only** son."*[88]

Isaac was not, at the time, Abraham's only son;[89] but he was Abraham's unique son. He was the one son God had promised

---

[86] Romans 5:8, RSV.
[87] Ephesians 5:2, RSV.
[88] Hebrews 11:17, RSV.
[89] Genesis 16:15-16.

Abraham, and the one through whom all the promises of God to Abraham were to be fulfilled.[90]

Is this Son of God in John 3:16 the only Son of God? In one sense, no—if we are to believe John when he says in Chapter 1, *"...to all who received him, to those who believed in his name, [he] gave the right to become children of God."*[91]

But Jesus is surely the *unique* Son of God—there is no one remotely like Him. Jesus is the unique Son, like (but even more than) Isaac was. And the heavenly Father of Jesus gave Him as a sacrificial offering, just Isaac's father would offer Isaac up.[92]

What does John 3:16 mean?

Let's go to Genesis 22 and see.

❧

There they are, Abraham and Isaac, climbing up a mountain, five hundred years before Moses will deliver the snake-bite survivors to the Promised Land, and two or three hundred more before Solomon will build a temple on the mount in Jerusalem[93] that tradition says is the very one this father and his son are climbing.

God has said to Abraham, *"Take your son, your only son Isaac, whom you love...and offer him...as a burnt offering."*[94]

And Abraham takes Isaac, his pride and joy and hope for the future, and prepares to give this "only" son—this unique, like-no-other son—as a sacrifice to God, because he loves God and trusts God more than he loves this special son whom he loves more than anything else in the world.

Abraham so loved God, that he gave his only son, Isaac. Abraham gave his son, but God did not take that son as a sacrifice.

---

[90] Genesis 17:18-21.
[91] John 1:12.
[92] Genesis 22:1-3.
[93] 2 Chronicles 3:1.
[94] Genesis 22:1, NRSV.

It turns out that Abraham is prophetic when he tells his son, *"God will provide himself a lamb for an offering."*[95]

God provides a ram for Abraham to sacrifice in place of Isaac. And God will come back to that place, far beyond Abraham's future, and provide another Lamb as a sacrificial offering. What God will not require of Abraham, He will do Himself for all the spiritual descendants of Abraham.[96] Though He spared Abraham's unique and beloved son, God will not spare His own Son, but will give Him up, offer Him up, for us all.[97]

God will love the world by giving His only, unique, like-no-other Son—because God is a Father Who loves the world—sinful and smitten men and women—you and me and everybody else—more than He loves the life of His own Son.

John 3:16 says that God has done what He commanded—but did not ultimately require—"Father" Abraham to do: God sacrificed His own special Son.

⤳⤶

But why would God conform His sacrifice of His Son to the image of Abraham giving up—offering up—Isaac?

For the same reason that God would require His Son to be lifted up as Moses lifted up that symbol of salvation in the Wilderness: so that those who know the stories will see the similarities—the parallels—and understand the meaning of those simple, all-too-familiar words: *"For God so loved the world that he gave his only begotten Son...."*

You know what it says. Do you know what it means?

Isaac was bound and helpless under the knife, but he did not die. The children of Israel, the descendants of Abraham and Isaac, were victims of the vipers, suffering for their sin, and they received

---

95 Genesis 22:8, NRSV.
96 Romans 4:13-25.
97 Romans 8:32.

life when death was their due. They saw the symbol of their salvation, a figure lifted up, taking their place.

৵৽

And here He is again. The Lamb is lifted up. The Son of God is given up. *"And whosoever believes in him shall not perish,"* any more than Isaac did on the mountain, or the children of Israel did looking up at the serpent. *"Whosoever believes in him shall not perish but have everlasting life."*

That's what it says.

And what does it mean?

It means eternal, everlasting life—for you and me and everybody who believes.

It means life.

৵৽

1 John 4:7-11 ESV

⁷ Beloved, let us love one another, for love is from God, and whoever loves has been born of God and knows God. ⁸ Anyone who does not love does not know God, because God is love. ⁹ In this the love of God was made manifest among us, that God sent his only Son into the world, so that we might live through him. ¹⁰ In this is love, not that we have loved God but that he loved us and sent his Son to be the propitiation for our sins. ¹¹ Beloved, if God so loved us, we also ought to love one another.

❧

John 3:16-21 ESV

[Jesus said:]

¹⁶ "For God so loved the world, that he gave his only Son, that whoever believes in him should not perish but have eternal life. ¹⁷ For God did not send his Son into the world to condemn the world, but in order that the world might be saved through him. ¹⁸ Whoever believes in him is not condemned, but whoever does not believe is condemned already, because he has not believed in the name of the only Son of God. ¹⁹ And this is the judgment: the light has come into the world, and people loved the darkness rather than the light because their works were evil. ²⁰ For everyone who does wicked things hates the light and does not come to the light, lest his works should be exposed. ²¹ But whoever does what is true comes to the light, so that it may be clearly seen that his works have been carried out in God."

❧

9.

What God Is

1 John 4:7-11; John 3:16-21 ESV

Sometimes, a church just needs to go back and review the basics. The Letter of 1ˢᵗ John was written to a church that needed to be reminded of—and recalled to—the fundamentals of our faith.

And fundamental to our faith is this simple truth: *"God is love."* The church that loses sight of this truth, and its implications, may be many things—and some of them very impressive—but it ceases to be a church—or soon will. And with so much going on in the life of a church and in the lives of its members and in the wider world around it, it is remarkably easy for a church to forget that *"God is love"* and what that reality means for us.

So, today, we review the basics of being an authentic church.

❧

Just as the old spiritual warned: "Everybody talking about heaven ain't going there,"[98] every group of people claiming to be a church ain't one—aren't one—isn't one—well, you get the point.

---

[98] "All God's Children Got Shoes," traditional American Spiritual.

We are not a church because we filled out the necessary legal papers or picked a name or started holding services—or bought a building. We are not a church because we have our theology and doctrine right or stay real busy doing religious things. We are not a church because we put on our best clothes and our best manners when we show up here on Sundays.

We are a real church when we love each other. We are a real church when we love each other with real love.

And if you're sitting there, proudly thinking, "That's us, all right! We are a real loving church!" I suggest you curb your enthusiasm until we unpack what the Bible means when it says we are to *"love one another."*

I think you will find that humility rather than pride is in order, no matter how much you think of your church. When you understand the standard that we are to be judged by, you will see that no church loves as well as it should—or could. Churches are made up of real people and real people are particularly hard for other real people to really love.

Really love.... What does that mean in the context of a church?

ॐ⊷ঌ

Well, first of all, throw out everything the world means by the word "love." Forget about "the desire to possess." Forget about natural responses to positive stimulation—the pleasure you feel when people are nice to you and things go the way you want them to or think they should.

The love that makes a group of people a church is what John is talking about when he says that *"God is love."* So it is not *our* love—it is *God's* love—that makes us a church. It is love that originates in God—that God generates. It is love that is a part of the essential character of God.

We may receive it. We may respond to it. We may express it. We may exercise it. But it is always a reality that comes to us from God. It did not start with us. Real love is God's love.

That's why it says, *"In this is love, not that we have loved God but that he loved us."*

We did not become Christians by deciding to love God or other people. We did not become a church by deciding to act lovingly toward each other or even toward God. We simply are not able to pull it off—even with the best effort at love we could possibly come up with.

It was God Who loved us. And we became aware of that love, and we accepted it, and put our faith in it and became something essentially different because of that love in us—which also enables us to know God in ways we did not know Him before we accepted His love—which makes this remarkable relationship we now have with God possible, individually and collectively—which makes us a church—His church—the church of the God Who is love.

࿇

And lest there be any confusion about what this love is like in real, down-to-earth, human terms, here's the paradigm: *"God so loved the world, that he gave his only Son, that whoever believes in him should not perish but have eternal life."*

That's the Gospel version. Here's how John puts it in the epistle: *"...the love of God was made manifest* [apparent—real—visible] *among us, that God sent his only Son into the world, so that we might live through him. He loved us and sent his Son to be the propitiation* [the atoning sacrifice—the substituted victim] *for our sins."*

God is love. Therefore, love is in the very nature of God— which means love is what God does—which means everything that God does is an act of love—everything! And the ultimate expression of God's love is God sacrificing His Son Jesus to wipe away the condemnation attached to our sins. The love of God is the act of giving up what one would naturally most want to have or hold on to. This love—this real love because it is God's love— is a love that is willing to suffer—even and especially unjustly and

67

innocently—in order to bring another into right relationship with the God Who loves that person as much as He loves us.

How do we know that is the nature of God's real love?

It's what He did for us in Jesus.

Can we love one another that way—with that kind of love?

That's what God wants from His church—from this church.

Do you begin to see why humility is in order?

෨·ஏ

When you walk into this sanctuary, that's the kind of love that awaits you from God—and the kind of love God expects you to show each other. When you do some underappreciated ministry for the umpteenth time—when you're confronted by a crisis you did not create—when you disagree with someone's theology or you're disappointed by someone's behavior (or embarrassed by your own)—when you find yourself typing an angry email—when you feel compelled to complain about something or somebody—God loves you still with His godly love and gives you that same kind of love to show everyone else—if you will.

Will you sacrifice yourself and your desires and your pride for this poor fellowship of sinners God sacrificed His Son for? Will we love one another in this church with real God-love, and, in that way, truly *be* a church? *Can* we love one another?

We can want to. We can at least try. We can do our best to take the love God has shown us—His love, not ours—and point it at each other.

What else can we do?

If we don't at least try to love one another, the Bible says we do not love God—whatever we may say to the contrary. And whatever problems we have with each other, we certainly have no "beefs" with God Who sent Jesus to die to save us—and showers us with love every day.

But look on the bright side: Any effort to love each other is going to please God. Anything we do to "do" like God will get

God's blessing and His empowerment. Every act of sacrificial love you direct toward a brother or sister in this fellowship will confirm the presence of God among us. Every act of sacrificial love will confirm to you that you are born again by God's love—and that God loves you.

When we love one another, we get closer to God and get to know Him better. When we love one another, God makes the love with which we love more fully His love.

৯৽৽৶

If all of this is true—and the Bible says it is bedrock truth—let me ask you a question: What do you suppose the impact of your loving others in this church could be on the rest of your life experience away from Trinity? What does how you relate to us have to do with the person you are and are becoming?

Ok—it was *two* questions. So here's two or three more: If we love each other more, are we more likely to become more loving— is God likely to *help* us be more loving—everywhere else? And would that please God? And would it please you?

If we don't love each other—even and especially when we have the most desire and (perhaps) justification *not* to—as far as God is concerned, we don't love Him, either. We can tell God how much we love Him all day long and well into the night, but if we don't love each other, He won't believe us, because God defines love for Him as loving the people He loves, whether they deserve it or not. When we don't *want* to is when we *need* to most.

৯৽৽৶

Here's a little mental exercise: If there is anybody in this church who bugs you—or has aggravated you—or has actually mistreated or hurt you—imagine you are holding his or her picture in your hand right now. If you need to look down at your hand to help you concentrate, that's okay.

Now imagine God loving that person—because you know God does. Now imagine that instead of that person's face in your imaginary picture in your hand, you substitute the face of Jesus. You can do this; it's your imagination. If it seems weird, remember that Jesus substituted Himself for each of us on the Cross, because God loves us—even the person in your mental picture.

Do you love Jesus?

Guess what. God wants you to love that other person the same way you love your Savior.

Is the idea of loving that person with the love of God easier if you see Jesus when you look at him or her? I hope so, because that's Who God sees when He looks at all of us.

What did John say? *"Beloved, if God so loved us, we also ought to love one another."*

"Beloved, let us love one another"—let us love one another, and be the church God loves.

ॐ✦ॐ

John 4:5-15a ESV

In the Gospel of John, Jesus infused the most basic things of life with deep spiritual meaning and made them symbols of divine truth. Water was one of those commonplace things that became an image of God's amazing grace for a woman who lived with a profound thirst for God.

ॐ

⁵ So [Jesus] came to a town of Samaria called Sychar, near the field that Jacob had given to his son Joseph. ⁶ Jacob's well was there; so Jesus, wearied as he was from his journey, was sitting beside the well. It was about the sixth hour.

⁷ A woman from Samaria came to draw water. Jesus said to her, "Give me a drink." ⁸ (For his disciples had gone away into the city to buy food.) ⁹ The Samaritan woman said to him, "How is it that you, a Jew, ask for a drink from me, a woman of Samaria?" (For Jews have no dealings with Samaritans.) ¹⁰ Jesus answered her, "If you knew the gift of God, and who it is that is saying to you, 'Give me a drink,' you would have asked him, and he would have given you living water." ¹¹ The woman said to him, "Sir, you have nothing to draw water with, and the well is deep. Where do you get that living water? ¹² Are you greater than our father Jacob? He gave us the well and drank from it himself, as did his sons and his livestock." ¹³ Jesus said to her, "Everyone who drinks of this water will be thirsty again, ¹⁴ but whoever drinks of the water that I will give him will never be thirsty again. The water that I will give him will become in him a spring of water welling up to eternal life." ¹⁵ The woman said to him, "Sir, give me this water, so that I will not be thirsty or have to come here to draw water."

ॐ

10.

Jesus Water

John 4:5-15 ESV

"Making your way in the world today
takes everything you've got.
Taking a break from all your worries
sure would help a lot.
Wouldn't you like to get away?"[99]

৯৯

These are not my words. I'm quoting—from the theme song
of a popular TV show that aired some 20 years ago. The words
continue:

"Sometimes you want to go
where everybody knows your name,
and they're always glad you came."[100]

The TV show was called "*Cheers*," a comedy about people who
spent their time—and their lives—in a popular Boston bar.

৯৯

---

[99] Gary Portnoy and Judy Hart-Angelo, "Where Everybody Knows Your
Name," theme song from the TV comedy series, *Cheers*, 1982-1993.
[100] Ibid.

73

And the connection with the woman at the well in Samaria?

Well, a bar is sometimes called a "watering hole."

But beyond that, there's more contrast than similarity. The woman who came to the watering hole outside the Samaritan village to fill her bucket at high noon would like to have "taken a break from all her worries"—would like very much to have "gotten away," as the song suggests.

But for her, "getting away" would have meant the opposite of what it did for the *Cheers* crowd. She would have wanted to go where *nobody* knew her name, because where she lived, they were never "glad she came."

Here was a woman who was at the low end of every pecking order. Ethnically, in a region where Jews despised Samaritans, she was a Samaritan. In a patriarchal culture where men dominated women, she was a woman. In a time when marriage established what status a woman had, she was not married—and, in fact, may have been divorced—and dishonored—by as many as five former husbands.

She was far enough down the economic ladder that she could not afford a servant to draw water for her. And in a village where the social network was everything, she was alone—ostracized—forced to fend for herself in the most basic chores of life, without help or fellowship.

She was reduced to depending on an unrelated man to provide for and protect her. No father, brother, son or other family member had taken her into his home as an unmarried woman should be. Who wouldn't want to get away from a life like hers?

And the well outside the town was the place she went every day to get away—even though it meant hard work in the hot sun, pulling the water up from deep down in the well and filling up a heavy pot that she would then have to haul back up the hill to the hut that was not her own. For those few minutes alone at the well, she could take a mental and emotional break—if not a physical one—from her unwanted way in the world.

She probably wouldn't have come at all—wouldn't have stepped outside the place where she lived—ever—if she didn't have to. But you have to have water to live—and so she came.

There was a time when Jesus was tempted in the desert and He said, *"Man shall not live on bread alone."*[101] And beside a well in Samaria, He showed that "woman" doesn't live on water alone, either. Not by *water* water—regular water—the world's water.

You see, there is "water"—and there is "Jesus Water." And a woman whose name we do not know—though everyone in the village did—is about to discover the difference.

The woman comes to the well for her water—everyday water. And on this day, there is a Man there—a Stranger Who has never been there before. And before she can turn around and march back up to town—which she surely would have done when she realized He was there—the strange Man speaks to her, which is stranger still.

He says, not "Give Me a drink," but "*Will you* give Me a drink?"

Sometimes Jesus tells people what to do, but other times, He asks people curious questions. He asked a blind man, *"What do you want Me to do for you?"*[102] He asked a man who had been crippled for decades, *"Do you want to get well?"*[103] And to a woman from whom the world had taken everything, Jesus puts the question: "Will you give Me something—something as simple as a drink of water—once you've drawn it up from the well?"

But even giving a stranger a drink of water when you're both standing right next to a well is not as simple as it sounds—for this particular woman. The woman says, "How could I do that even if I were willing? Your Jewish rules won't let You touch anything I've touched. Why do You ask me for what You couldn't take even if I

---

[101] Luke 4:4, NIV.
[102] Mark 10:51, RSV.
[103] John 5:6, NIV.

would give it?" She knows it's not possible. She cannot give a Jewish man water.

But there is something she does not know. She does not know Who this particular Jewish Man is, or what He is able and willing to give to her.

But she is about to find out.

And when she does, she will—finally—get away from the way her life is going and all the worries that fill it—because that's what happens when you get filled with "Jesus Water."

It turns out that she doesn't need everybody to know her name. Just Jesus. And He knows, not just her name, but, as she will soon discover, everything about her.

And knowing everything about her, He still wants to give her "living water—never-thirst-again water—a spring of water welling up to eternal life." In short: "Jesus Water."

But she is confused. What does this Stranger—this maybe-the-Messiah—mean? What is His "living water"?

⇛⇝

It's a symbol, of course. You have to have water to live—even today—even if you get yours from the tap or the store, instead of a well outside of town. You have to have water to live; it's a basic biological truth.

But there is an equally basic spiritual truth: You have a spiritual life—a part of who you are—the ultimate essence of who you are. And that spiritual life thirsts for God the way your body thirsts for water. You must have God to live. God meets your primal spiritual thirst—if you let Him—by filling you with His divine Spirit. God matches your spirit's need with what meets that need, just like cool water quenches a burning thirst.

You can substitute other things for God to try to get rid of your spiritual thirst—and many people do. But it is like drinking salt water instead of fresh water. It feels like what you need at the time, but it soon makes the thirst even worse.

Can we define it any better than that?

Not really. Living water—basic spiritual sustenance—is what God gives that we need Him to give us. He gives it through what He did in Jesus when Jesus lived on earth and went to places like that town in Samaria and talked to people like the woman at the well.

But here's how it works: Jesus asks you, "Will you give Me what I ask from you?" and you get to ask Him, "Give me this 'living water' so that it will do for me spiritually what I need God to do."

What we do know is that Jesus has this living spiritual "water"—this power of God for your life—to give. And if you want it and will receive it from Him, He will give it to you, and it will change the spiritual part of your life so that the spiritual part makes all the other parts whole and full and rich, in life itself.

⊷⊶

So here's another story: A Stranger shows up at another watering hole—a modern watering hole, like, say, a bar in Boston—where everybody knows everybody's name, but nobody seems to know His. They're all drinking something—filling their pots, so to speak—and they all seem happy. The place is a laugh a minute.

Except that what they're drinking—physically and spiritually—will not quench the thirst of the soul. And the Stranger goes from stool to stool, looking into every man's and woman's heart and saying, "Come drink with Me. Come drink the living water that fills you with what is missing inside you."

How many, do you think, will put down what they've been "putting down" and switch to what the Stranger Who is Jesus offers, instead?

Living water is a symbol for the presence and power of the Holy Spirit provided by Jesus Christ to unite us and our lives with God the Father.

Cheers is a symbol of this world, with all the options it makes available to all the people who are trying to quench a spiritual thirst with everything but the one Thing that will get the job done.

After a lifetime of spiritual thirst, like the woman at the well, "sometimes you want to go where *Jesus* knows your name, and He's always glad you came."

But, of course, for that, you've got to know *His* Name, and you've got to be glad *He* came. When you know *His* Name and welcome His coming into your life, the living water is yours for the asking. The "Jesus Water" will spring up within you, filling you forever with eternal life, quenching that thirst in your soul that nothing else can.

What did she say?

"Sir, give me this water!"

That's all it takes.

Drink up!

જ⊶⊰

John 6:1-21 NRSV

[1] *After this Jesus went to the other side of the Sea of Galilee, also called the Sea of Tiberias.* [2] *A large crowd kept following him, because they saw the signs that he was doing for the sick.* [3] *Jesus went up the mountain and sat down there with his disciples.* [4] *Now the Passover, the festival of the Jews, was near.* [5] *When he looked up and saw a large crowd coming toward him, Jesus said to Philip, "Where are we to buy bread for these people to eat?"* [6] *He said this to test him, for he himself knew what he was going to do.* [7] *Philip answered him, "Six months' wages would not buy enough bread for each of them to get a little."* [8] *One of his disciples, Andrew, Simon Peter's brother, said to him,* [9] *"There is a boy here who has five barley loaves and two fish. But what are they among so many people?"* [10] *Jesus said, "Make the people sit down." Now there was a great deal of grass in the place; so they sat down, about five thousand in all.* [11] *Then Jesus took the loaves, and when he had given thanks, he distributed them to those who were seated; so also the fish, as much as they wanted.* [12] *When they were satisfied, he told his disciples, "Gather up the fragments left over, so that nothing may be lost."* [13] *So they gathered them up, and from the fragments of the five barley loaves, left by those who had eaten, they filled twelve baskets.* [14] *When the people saw the sign that he had done, they began to say, "This is indeed the prophet who is to come into the world."*

[15] *When Jesus realized that they were about to come and take him by force to make him king, he withdrew again to the mountain by himself.*

[16] *When evening came, his disciples went down to the sea,* [17] *got into a boat, and started across the sea to Capernaum. It was now dark, and Jesus had not yet come to them.* [18] *The sea became rough because a strong wind was blowing.* [19] *When they had rowed about three or four miles, they saw Jesus walking on the sea and coming near the boat, and they were terrified.* [20] *But he said to them, "It is I; do not be afraid."* [21] *Then they wanted to take him into the boat, and immediately the boat reached the land toward which they were going.*

❧◦❧

11.

The Miracle in the Middle

John 6:1-21 NRSV

In the Gospel reading we just heard, there are two amazing, miraculous events. The passage begins with Jesus hosting an impromptu picnic for five thousand people and feeding them all with next to no food. The passage ends with Jesus walking on the water across the Sea of Galilee to join a bumpy boat ride already in progress.

Miracles both, certainly—and so spectacular that you could be forgiven for not noticing that there is a third miracle in the passage—the miracle in the middle—a quiet little miracle sandwiched in between the two dramatic demonstrations of the power that Jesus bore in His body and brought to the people of God.

After the disciples gathered up the leftovers from the lunch on the lawn, and before they got underway for a little nighttime navigation, Jesus—according to the scriptures—realized that His five thousand very satisfied dinner guests *"were about to come and take him by force and make him king."*

That He realized this may or may not be a miracle (we don't know what they were saying or doing). But His reaction definitely was. When Jesus realized what they had in mind, *"He withdrew again to the mountain by himself."* And that, my friends, is a miracle, and every bit as amazing, in its own way, as the other ones in the passage.

After all, Jesus came into the world to be a king. He told Pilate as much.[104] The Bible tells us over and over that Jesus was a descendent of David, Israel's greatest king.[105] And goodness knows, they needed a king and wanted one. And now they're ready to make Jesus their king.

But Jesus, the true King of the Jews, will have nothing to do with this mob of Jews wanting to take Him and make Him their king. From a human perspective, it's incredible. To get some idea of how incredible, consider this: After leading the ragtag colonists to independence in the American Revolution, George Washington, at the peak of his power and prestige, simply resigned his commission and went home to private life. The British king, Washington's old enemy, is reported to have said in response to the news, "If he does that, he will be the greatest man in the world."[106]

How can you pass up the role of ruler when it's right there for the taking?

Jesus wanted to be their king. God wanted Jesus to be their king. These Jews are trying to make Jesus their king. And Jesus "withdraws."

What's the problem?

The problem is that just as Jesus will not be bought off by the devil in the desert with a deceptive promise of kingship, so He will not allow Himself here to be taken by force and made a king, however well-intentioned the "takers" are.

---

[104] John 18:36-37.

[105] Matthew 1:1.

[106] The king supposedly made the comment to his court painter, Benjamin West, in 1783, who reported it in a letter dated May 3, 1797, to Rufus King, an American minister to Great Britain, who preserved the letter in his memorandum book.

You cannot "take" Jesus. He will not allow it. You can only receive Him. You cannot "make" Him king; He is already King. You can only acknowledge His Lordship on His terms.

A person in high position—even one as high as a king—is subject to whoever put him in that position. If they make Jesus king, He is subject to them, even as king. The only kingmaker Jesus is willing to submit to is His Heavenly Father. God's hand is the only hand from which Jesus will accept a crown.

Have you ever noticed how when you want to use Jesus to meet some pressing personal agenda—when you want Jesus to solve some vexing problem in your life your way—Jesus has this tendency to withdraw—to become unavailable for the task you would assign Him?

You cannot "take and make" Jesus, whether by physical force or emotional manipulation or any other methodology that would require Him to be subject to you in any way.

The Jesus Who will be present to you under any and every circumstance as your Sovereign Lord[107] will not accept any other position. He will not fill any role in your life except that which His Heavenly Father has assigned Him.

Submit yourself fully to Jesus and He will come and be Your Savior and King. Make Him anything else in your life, and He won't be there at all. Jesus will walk away from any deal contrary to His Heavenly Father's will.

It's amazing how that works: Take and make?

No way.

Receive and acknowledge?

And there is your King.

It's a miracle, really.

৵৽

---

107 Matthew 28:19-20.

John 6:35, 41-51 NRSV

[35] Jesus said to them, "I am the bread of life. Whoever comes to me will never be hungry, and whoever believes in me will never be thirsty.

[41] Then the Jews began to complain about him because he said, "I am the bread that came down from heaven." [42] They were saying, "Is not this Jesus, the son of Joseph, whose father and mother we know? How can he now say, 'I have come down from heaven'?" [43] Jesus answered them, "Do not complain among yourselves. [44] No one can come to me unless drawn by the Father who sent me; and I will raise that person up on the last day. [45] It is written in the prophets, 'And they shall all be taught by God.' Everyone who has heard and learned from the Father comes to me. [46] Not that anyone has seen the Father except the one who is from God; he has seen the Father. [47] Very truly, I tell you, whoever believes has eternal life. [48] I am the bread of life. [49] Your ancestors ate the manna in the wilderness, and they died. [50] This is the bread that comes down from heaven, so that one may eat of it and not die. [51] I am the living bread that came down from heaven. Whoever eats of this bread will live forever; and the bread that I will give for the life of the world is my flesh."

۞e

12.

Hunger and Thirst

John 6:35, 41-51 NRSV

The Bible was translated from the original languages into English hundreds of years ago. New translations, in English, turn up in the books stores all the time. But even when you recognize the words in the Bible as familiar English words, the ideas they convey may still be very foreign.

For instance, do you think the words of Jesus about His being the Bread of life are going to mean the same thing to people who take every meal for granted as they did to people who were never very far from starvation? Jesus is talking to people who may not know where their next meal is coming from. They only know their last one came from Him. And so they want to stay close to Jesus—to get fed—literally.

Hungry people—these people—aren't that concerned with graphic metaphors of deep spiritual truths. The bread they want to know about is, well, bread—real live daily bread.

It's not that God can't take a hand in giving them bread. He dropped bread out of heaven on their ancestors in the wilderness, according to the Bible.[108] They would be willing to support a similar

---

[108] Exodus 16.

food distribution plan at present, if God chose to revive the "manna-from-heaven" program for them.

So they perk up when the Jesus-Who-feeds-the-multitudes-with-food-that-didn't-exist-a-moment-before claims to be God's Bread from heaven. Hungry people want to be fed. Thirsty people want to drink.

Jesus, the Living Water, gave them to drink. Jesus, the Bread of life, fed them. But it wasn't their physical hunger Jesus came to feed; it wasn't a physical thirst Jesus meant to quench. These people were *spiritually* malnourished and didn't even recognize it—most of them.

They certainly didn't want to hear about some fanciful ideas like a local carpenter's son being the long-promised Messianic Savior of the world.[109] That, for them, was an absolutely foreign concept, no matter how clear and familiar the words were.

You may find the idea of spiritual hunger easier to understand than physical hunger. Do you hunger or thirst for anything in this life? Is there a spiritual appetite inside that yearns to be nourished by the Bread from heaven?

Amazing, isn't it, when your physical hunger is always met completely—often instantaneously—when you become aware of it—and yet there are other hungers and thirsts of a different, but no less significant, type, that linger, not just for an hour or two, but for months and years and lifetimes. These are the hungers and thirsts that are as familiar to the modern "palate" as they were to the people of Jesus' day and before—more so, perhaps. These are the hungers and thirsts that our world calls social or psychological, socio-economic, ethnic or political. They are all, in the end, spiritual.

Feed them all with pleasure or power or prestige or possessions or professional success, and the hunger is still there. The thirst for

---

[109] Matthew 13:53-58.

more of what this world has to offer will not be quenched with more of what this world has to offer.

And so Jesus offers to feed the hungry and provide for the thirsty. He sets up no soup kitchens—worthy and valuable as they are. Massive dinners on the ground become a thing of the past. Jesus feeds all who come to Him and believe in Him by putting something very foreign on the menu—something unimaginably exotic—something absolutely heavenly: Bread from heaven—and living, heavenly Water.

And He invites everyone to dinner—this heavenly dinner— where everyone who comes is fed by "Jesus food" that takes all these spiritual hungers away.

You weren't there when the bread fell out of heaven in the desert. You weren't there when Jesus multiplied the loaves by the lake in Galilee. But you are here now, today, with all the spiritual hungers the delights of this world cannot satisfy.

And here is Jesus, offering to feed you, with the most foreign and filling food you could ever—or never—imagine: Jesus Himself—the Bread of life. Don't pass up this invitation. *"Oh taste and see,"* as the Psalmist says, *"that the Lord is good."*

తం•ఈ

> *I will praise the Lord at all times,*
> *I will constantly speak his praises.*
> *O, taste and see that the Lord is good.*
> *Even strong young lions*
> *sometimes go hungry,*
> *but those who trust in the Lord*
> *will lack no good thing.*[110]

తం•ఈ

---

[110] Psalm 34:1, 8, 10, NLT.

Psalm 23 KJV

[1] *The LORD is my shepherd; I shall not want.*

[2] *He maketh me to lie down in green pastures:*
he leadeth me beside the still waters.

[3] *He restoreth my soul:*
he leadeth me in the paths of righteousness for his name's sake.

[4] *Yea, though I walk through the valley of the shadow of death,*
I will fear no evil: for thou art with me;
thy rod and thy staff they comfort me.

[5] *Thou preparest a table before me in the presence of mine enemies:*
thou anointest my head with oil; my cup runneth over.

[6] *Surely goodness and mercy shall follow me all the days of my life:*
and I will dwell in the house of the LORD for ever.

෧෨

John 10:1-11 RSV

[Jesus said:]

¹ "Truly, truly, I say to you, he who does not enter the sheepfold by the door but climbs in by another way, that man is a thief and a robber; ² but he who enters by the door is the shepherd of the sheep. ³ To him the gatekeeper opens; the sheep hear his voice, and he calls his own sheep by name and leads them out. ⁴ When he has brought out all his own, he goes before them, and the sheep follow him, for they know his voice. ⁵ A stranger they will not follow, but they will flee from him, for they do not know the voice of strangers." ⁶ This figure Jesus used with them, but they did not understand what he was saying to them.

⁷ So Jesus again said to them, "Truly, truly, I say to you, I am the door of the sheep. ⁸ All who came before me are thieves and robbers; but the sheep did not heed them. ⁹ I am the door; if any one enters by me, he will be saved, and will go in and out and find pasture. ¹⁰ The thief comes only to steal and kill and destroy; I came that they may have life, and have it abundantly. ¹¹ I am the good shepherd. The good shepherd lays down his life for the sheep."

☙❧

13.

Sheep and Their Shepherd

Psalm 23 KJV; John 10:1-11 RSV

The 23rd Psalm is the most famous psalm in the Bible, and almost certainly the most popular. It is also the most powerful, mending broken hearts at gravesides and sustaining failing hearts overwhelmed by crisis or awash in fear.

The psalm is compelling because it is simple:

"The Lord is my shepherd..."

That metaphor—that image—confronts you, and then the Psalmist unpacks it: *"The Lord is my shepherd* and because of that, I—lack—nothing! Every hunger—every thirst—is provided for. No dark moment is faced alone. No danger goes unchallenged."

"This is what I have experienced," says the Psalmist. "This is what I know."

And you know what? Across the centuries—across the globe—men and women who read it or hear it or memorize it don't say, "That's ridiculous!" They say, "That's right! Me, too! The Lord is my Shepherd. That's how I see things, too."

It's helpful—comforting—to have an image like a shepherd to look to when you're trying to imagine God. I'd much rather my God be a protecting, providing Presence than an angry, vengeful Judge or a cold and distant Mystery.

But to say that God is your Shepherd is also to say at the same time—or at least to imply—the other part of the equation: I am His sheep. It seems like an obvious next step in our understanding of things, but not all obvious steps get taken. Too many people don't make the sheep-and-shepherd, me-and-God, connection. They choose other animal analogies to embody their self-perception. Let me illustrate:

Some of you have cats as pets, and some of you have dogs. We all know they're very different animals. They seem to have very different perspectives. Someone has said that the difference is that a dog thinks: "This person feeds me and keeps me warm and comfortable. This person showers me with affection and attends to all my wants. This person must be a *god*."

On the other hand, the cat thinks: "This person feeds me and keeps me warm and comfortable. This person showers me with affection and attends to all my wants. *I* must be a god."

In your relationship with God, it's important to know who's who. Who's the god and who's the "pet"? Who's the sheep and Who's the Shepherd?

The Psalmist says, "God takes me where I can eat and drink my fill. God provides me with moral guidance and spiritual renewal. God protects me from evil so effectively that even when I see it everywhere, I'm not afraid. He heals my wounds and makes me confident that what is to come in life will be even better than what I have experienced so far."

"The best way I know to describe what I have experienced," says the Psalmist, "is that this Provider and Protector is a God Who behaves toward me like a shepherd. What I experience is what sheep experience when a shepherd provides and protects them. Simply put: 'The Lord is my Shepherd; I am His sheep.'"

So far, so good. If you know that much, you know something important.

✦

But compared to what else there is to know, it really isn't much. Knowing something about God is good: God is like a shepherd to me. But imagine how much more there is to know!

A small-town newspaper carried a human-interest story about a 94-year old woman in a local nursing home and her daughter who came every day to be with her. The daughter, herself a senior citizen, lovingly combed her mother's hair and washed her face. She rolled her mother's wheelchair to the lunch room where she helped the elderly woman eat her food. This daughter hugged her mother and kissed her every day as she had done for so many, many years, and yet the mother's mind was so dim and her understanding so limited that she could only describe this one who loved her and provided for her most basic needs as "that lady who feeds me." That's all she knew.

But there was so much more.

What do sheep know about their relationship with their shepherd? Not much, really.

I am God's sheep. God is my Shepherd. God leads me, feeds me, protects me, provides for me and promises me a life rich in goodness and mercy. That's enough to justify the "shepherd" metaphor.

But Who is this shepherd God? Who is this mysterious Presence, this great and benevolent Power. Who is this God?

For the answer to that question, we have to look beyond the 23rd Psalm. Psalm 23 provides us the human perspective on a person's relationship with God.

Inspired?

Certainly.

Powerful?

Without a doubt.

But there is a difference between the human perspective and the divine perspective. For the divine perspective, we have to go to the New Testament—to the Gospel of John.

ॐॐ

In John, Chapter 4, Jesus said to a woman He met at a well, *"If you knew...who it is that is saying to you, 'Give me a drink,' you would have asked him and he would have given you living water."*[111]

Do you see the connection?

> *"The Lord is my shepherd...*
> *He leads me beside the still waters."*

In the tenth chapter of the Gospel of John, Jesus lays it out plainly. *"I am the good shepherd,"* He says. The Lord Who is our Shepherd is revealed to be not a mysterious, unknown deity, but a God Who *"became flesh and dwelled among us."*[112]

We, like sheep, could not know the God Who is our divine Shepherd if we only had our human senses and intuition to go by. But our Shepherd God could cause us to know what He wants us to know. It's called "revelation."

John said, *"No one has ever seen God, but the only Son...has made him known."*[113]

"The Lord is my shepherd," said the Psalmist.

"I am the good shepherd," said Jesus.

What a glorious discovery!

What a glorious revelation!

⤙⤚

Do you remember the movie, "You've Got Mail"?[114]

A young woman was communicating by email with someone who was always kind and compassionate. She savored every message she got from him because he somehow understood her in a way no one else did, and he seemed to know exactly what she needed to hear. She just didn't know who he was. He was a stranger: no name—no face.

---

[111] John 4:10, RSV.
[112] John 1:14.
[113] John 1:18, RSV.
[114] Movie *You've Got Mail!* 1998.

At the same time, she was confronted by someone who seemed to be an enemy. This man upended her world and made it impossible for her to live as she had before.

Gradually, however, she began to realize that this frustrating man with the familiar face and the famous name was not an enemy. She came to appreciate other things about him—good qualities. And yet, all the time, she yearned to know the identity of the other, unknown one who had been speaking so sweetly to her heart from the beginning.

And then one day, the person she had come to love more than anybody else revealed that he was also the mysterious stranger who had loved her all along.

Do you remember what she told him?

"I wanted it to be you!"

And while you are depending on the Lord Who is your Shepherd—Whoever He is—He announces to you that He is Jesus Christ.

"*I am the good shepherd,*" He says, "I made sure you lacked nothing. I made you lie down in green pastures. I led you beside still waters. I restored your soul. I led you in righteous paths even through dark valleys. Through all the hardships and difficulties—through all the uncertainties and sorrows—I protected you and provided for you and restored you. I am the Good Shepherd and I have proved it by laying down My life for you."

And can you say, "Oh, Jesus, I wanted it to be You"? Isn't This Who you wanted your God to be?

You can't be your own God. In this, if nothing else, cats are mistaken. A god has to be able to protect you and provide for you. Can you restore your own soul in a world like ours—in a life like yours?

You can tell Jesus, the Good Shepherd: "I want it to be You. I want the divine Shepherd Who has blessed me in so many ways all the days of my life to be the Savior Who gave His life, in love, for me. The Lord Jesus Christ is my Shepherd. His sheep am I."

Coming to this realization—accepting this revelation—is essential. Everyone is a sheep in comparison to God.

But, according to Jesus the Good Shepherd, not every sheep is His. Jesus says in John 10 that, in order to be His sheep, you have to hear His voice, know His voice, and follow Him.

He will go after stray sheep, of course. Even if you were the only one, He would leave the rest and come find you and bring you back to the safety of the fold.[115]

But

"All we like sheep have gone astray,"

says Isaiah,

"we have turned every one to his own way."[116]

So you're not the only one the Good Shepherd has had to rescue.

But remember, the Good Shepherd herds sheep, not cats. Do not think you are blessed because you deserve it.

Jesus calls His own sheep by name and leads them out, into this world and through it to the house of His Father. Do you hear His voice? Is the Lord Jesus Christ, the Good Shepherd, your Shepherd?

In the end, we're all sheep, really.

Whose sheep are you?

(BA)A-men.

෯෧

---

[115] Luke 15:3-7.
[116] Isaiah 53:6, RSV.

Isaiah 40:9-11 ESV

⁹ Go on up to a high mountain,
O Zion, herald of good news;
lift up your voice with strength,
O Jerusalem, herald of good news;
lift it up, fear not;
say to the cities of Judah,
"Behold your God!"
¹⁰ Behold, the Lord GOD comes with might,
and his arm rules for him;
behold, his reward is with him,
and his recompense before him.
¹¹ He will tend his flock like a shepherd;
he will gather the lambs in his arms;
he will carry them in his bosom,
and gently lead those that are with young.

৵৽

John 10:2-4, 7-11 ESV

[Jesus said:]

² But he who enters by the door is the shepherd of the sheep. ³ To him the gatekeeper opens. The sheep hear his voice, and he calls his own sheep by name and leads them out. ⁴ When he has brought out all his own, he goes before them, and the sheep follow him, for they know his voice.

⁷ So Jesus again said to them, "Truly, truly, I say to you, I am the door of the sheep. ⁸ All who came before me are thieves and robbers, but the sheep did not listen to them. ⁹ I am the door. If anyone enters by me, he will be saved and will go in and out and find pasture. ¹⁰ The thief comes only to steal and kill and destroy. I came that they may have life and have it abundantly. ¹¹ I am the good shepherd. The good shepherd lays down his life for the sheep."

৯০০৬

14.

Traits of a Shepherd

Isaiah 40:9-11; John 10:2-4, 7-11 ESV

Well, you heard the Gospel reading: Jesus said, *"I am the good shepherd."* You heard the words, but did you hear what He's saying.

Jesus isn't talking to His disciples, offering them the comforting reassurance these words have become for us throughout the ages. Jesus isn't talking to the crowds of curious, fascinated folks who don't know what to make of Him, but don't want to miss a minute of the show, either.

This is not an invitation to them to have faith in Him, though His whole life is such an invitation.

Jesus is talking to the religious leaders of His day—to Pharisees—and others—who have assigned themselves the role of "shepherds of the people of God." And His words are a direct and intentional challenge to their self-assumed authority over everybody else.

"*I* am the Good Shepherd," Jesus says. "Not you." "I am the *Good* Shepherd—as opposed to the kind of shepherds you have shown yourselves to be." "I am the Good Shepherd"—as opposed to—*what?*

Thieves and robbers, apparently—and wolves. If the shoe fits, fellows—wear it!

Jesus did not come into this world to be nice.[117] He did not give up His throne in heaven[118] to get along with everybody down here on earth. Jesus came to turn our world upside down[119]—to take over—and take back what really belongs to God[120]: the human race and the authority to say how people will live their lives in this world God created lovingly for them—for us.

"*I*—am the good Shepherd!"

Do you *hear* what He's saying?

All through the Bible—all through the history of Israel—there were shepherds. God's people started out as shepherds: *"My father was a wandering Aramean"* was the way the Hebrews' historic confession of faith began, referring to the Patriarch Abraham, who "wandered" into the Holy Land as the head shepherd of a huge flock of sheep and goats and the people who helped him tend them.[121]

Moses was the shepherd God appointed to lead His people out of Egypt,[122] just as Joshua was the shepherd who led them into the land of milk and honey.[123] David was the Shepherd King[124] (despite the business with Bathsheba[125]). And all those after him, in the palace and among the priests, fashioned themselves "shepherds" as well, except that prophet after prophet wouldn't let them get away with it, because time after time their performance failed to match the measure God set for them when He set them upon the throne—or before the altar—to shepherd His people.[126]

---

[117] Matthew 10:34.

[118] Philippians 2:6-7.

[119] Acts 17:6.

[120] Revelation 11:15.

[121] Deuteronomy 26:5, NIV.

[122] Exodus 3:1.

[123] Deuteronomy 3:28.

[124] 1 Chronicles 11:1-2.

[125] 2 Samuel 11.

[126] Isaiah 56:11; Jeremiah 10:21; Ezekiel 34:1-10; Zechariah 10:3.

Isaiah said, *"the Sovereign Lord...tends his flock like a shepherd."* Ezekiel wrote, *"'I myself will tend my sheep...,' declares the Sovereign Lord. '...I will shepherd the flock....'"*[127]

Okay, "the cat's out of the bag": According to the prophets, God is the Good Shepherd.

Like they say, "Other guys imitate us, but the original is still the greatest."

"I am the good shepherd," Jesus tells the Pharisees, who are none too happy with Him to start with. And you know this claim—in direct challenge to them—of divine authority and, apparently, to divinity as well—is not winning Him any converts among the "we're the ones who should get to tell everybody what to do" class.

☙❧

So what kind of a shepherd is Jesus claiming to be—besides "good"?

He's claiming to be the kind of shepherd that lays down His life for His sheep, which would be a pretty audacious claim, if we didn't know already that He makes good on it. And the point isn't that He dies. Everybody does that, sooner or later. And anybody can get himself killed, given the right—or wrong—circumstances.

The point—and power—of the claim is that Jesus will lay down His life—give His life voluntarily when He could do otherwise—for His sheep.

The Pharisees are the kind of folks who are willing to sacrifice, too—to sacrifice sheep—anybody in the flock—if they decide the individual deserves to be sacrificed—or if they think it necessary to avoid danger to themselves or the rest of the flock. After all, to them, the shepherd is far more important than his sheep and a lot of sheep are more important than any particular one.[128] Sheep are just sheep and "a shepherd's got to do what a shepherd's got to do."

---

127 Ezekiel 34:15-16, NIV.
128 But see Matthew 18:12-13.

Except that Jesus has a whole different take on the traits of a shepherd—a good shepherd.

Jesus understands what makes a good shepherd—*the* Good Shepherd—and knows that that is what God has sent Him to be. And so Jesus lays down His life for His sheep. Jesus lays down His life so the sheep don't have to lay theirs down, as they would have to if He were not there to die in their place. The Shepherd has the choice in this case; the sheep do not.

The Good Shepherd puts the wellbeing of the sheep before His own. He puts their lives before His own. It is an approach to shepherding that will turn the world upside down, which is the point.

Without the shepherd, the sheep die. With the shepherd, the sheep live. It is that simple and that stark. *"I came that they may have life.* I came that the sheep may have all the life they can possibly have."

But notice that not all the sheep are His. Not all the sheep belong to the Good Shepherd.

There are sheep that do not listen to His voice. They do not recognize Jesus as their Shepherd.

At least, that's what Jesus is telling the Pharisees. Makes you wonder who He's talking about.

But let's leave these other sheep where they are for a minute and look at the sheep Jesus claims as His own.

The Good Shepherd Who will lay down His life for His sheep so that they will live and not die knows them by name. And He calls them by name. And dumb as they are, they at least listen to their Shepherd's voice. And they recognize that voice as the voice of their Shepherd, and they follow Him.

"Do they follow Him because they understand everything He says to them?"

Don't be silly. They're sheep. They don't understand much at all, except that that is the voice they recognize as their Good Shepherd. They trust Him and they follow Him.

They follow their Shepherd to pasture and to safety. He provides for them and He protects them.

And even that they may not understand—they may not even know that's what the Shepherd is doing. But He's doing it, just the same, all the time.

And He is able to do it because they follow Him. He can and does protect and provide for any sheep that will hear His voice and follow Him.

And the others who put themselves forward as shepherds?

They neither provide nor protect. They can't. They are not shepherds.

↾↿

But how many people want you to think they are!

The Pharisees aren't the only supposed shepherds the Good Shepherd has to contend with. Look around at all the would-be shepherds maneuvering around the sheep today. Everybody wants to lead sheep. False shepherds sneak into the places where sheep await the real Shepherd and say whatever they can think of to coax the unsuspecting to listen to their voices instead of His and follow them to nowhere good.

And here's the funny thing: The pretend shepherds are really just sheep themselves. Jesus calls them, too, just like He calls His own sheep. But they will not hear Him. They will not recognize His voice or listen. Or if they do recognize His voice, they still don't listen, and the result is the same.

They are like the blind leading the blind, Jesus says: Everybody ends up in a ditch. [129]

---

[129] Matthew 15:14.

And when they do, the Good Shepherd goes and looks for them, even if it means leaving 99 in safety[130]—even if it means laying down His life to keep them from losing theirs. The Good Shepherd goes wherever the lost sheep goes. The Good Shepherd calls the name of the lost sheep, whoever it is. The Good Shepherd saves the life of the lost sheep, no matter how much danger the sheep got itself into. That's the Good Shepherd. That's Jesus.

જી-જ

But in the end, only the sheep that hear His voice and follow Him are His sheep. Jesus would be the Good Shepherd for any sheep. That's what He's here for. That's why He's turning the world upside down—still: looking for lost sheep to add to the flock that He protects and provides for. That's why He even bothers to tell this to Pharisees and other would-be, but counterfeit, shepherds. The Good Shepherd speaks to every sheep—no matter how rebellious—in hopes that His voice will be heard and recognized and trusted and followed.

"I am the good shepherd," Jesus tells the sheep who will not hear Him.

But for those who will, Jesus, in the words Isaiah uses of God,
> *"...tends his flock like a shepherd:*
> *He gathers the lambs in his arms*
> *and carries them close to his heart...*
> *the Sovereign Lord comes with power...*
> *and gently leads."*

Is the Lord your Shepherd?

જી-જ

---

[130] Matthew 18:12-13.

John 11:1-45 RSV

¹ *Now a certain man was ill, Laz'arus of Bethany, the village of Mary and her sister Martha.* ² *It was Mary who anointed the Lord with ointment and wiped his feet with her hair, whose brother Laz'arus was ill.* ³ *So the sisters sent to him, saying, "Lord, he whom you love is ill."* ⁴ *But when Jesus heard it he said, "This illness is not unto death; it is for the glory of God, so that the Son of God may be glorified by means of it."*

⁵ *Now Jesus loved Martha and her sister and Laz'arus.* ⁶ *So when he heard that he was ill, he stayed two days longer in the place where he was.* ⁷ *Then after this he said to the disciples, "Let us go into Judea again."* ⁸ *The disciples said to him, "Rabbi, the Jews were but now seeking to stone you, and are you going there again?"* ⁹ *Jesus answered, "Are there not twelve hours in the day? If any one walks in the day, he does not stumble, because he sees the light of this world.* ¹⁰ *But if any one walks in the night, he stumbles, because the light is not in him."* ¹¹ *Thus he spoke, and then he said to them, "Our friend Laz'arus has fallen asleep, but I go to awake him out of sleep."* ¹² *The disciples said to him, "Lord, if he has fallen asleep, he will recover."* ¹³ *Now Jesus had spoken of his death, but they thought that he meant taking rest in sleep.* ¹⁴ *Then Jesus told them plainly, "Laz'arus is dead;* ¹⁵ *and for your sake I am glad that I was not there, so that you may believe. But let us go to him."* ¹⁶ *Thomas, called the Twin, said to his fellow disciples, "Let us also go, that we may die with him."*

¹⁷ *Now when Jesus came, he found that Laz'arus had already been in the tomb four days.* ¹⁸ *Bethany was near Jerusalem, about two miles off,* ¹⁹ *and many of the Jews had come to Martha and Mary to console them concerning their brother.* ²⁰ *When Martha heard that Jesus was coming, she went and met him, while Mary sat in the house.* ²¹ *Martha said to Jesus, "Lord, if you had been here, my brother would not have died.* ²² *And even now I know that whatever you ask from God, God will give you."* ²³ *Jesus said to her, "Your brother will rise again."* ²⁴ *Martha said to him, "I know that he will rise again in the resurrection at the last day."* ²⁵ *Jesus said to her, "I am the resurrection and the life; he who believes in me, though he die, yet shall he live,* ²⁶ *and whoever lives and believes in me shall never die. Do you believe this?"*

²⁷ *She said to him, "Yes, Lord; I believe that you are the Christ, the Son of God, he who is coming into the world."*

²⁸ *When she had said this, she went and called her sister Mary, saying quietly, "The Teacher is here and is calling for you."* ²⁹ *And when she heard it, she rose quickly and went to him.* ³⁰ *Now Jesus had not yet come to the village, but was still in the place where Martha had met him.* ³¹ *When the Jews who were with her in the house, consoling her, saw Mary rise quickly and go out, they followed her, supposing that she was going to the tomb to weep there.* ³² *Then Mary, when she came where Jesus was and saw him, fell at his feet, saying to him, "Lord, if you had been here, my brother would not have died."* ³³ *When Jesus saw her weeping, and the Jews who came with her also weeping, he was deeply moved in spirit and troubled;* ³⁴ *and he said, "Where have you laid him?" They said to him, "Lord, come and see."* ³⁵ *Jesus wept.* ³⁶ *So the Jews said, "See how he loved him!"* ³⁷ *But some of them said, "Could not he who opened the eyes of the blind man have kept this man from dying?"*

³⁸ *Then Jesus, deeply moved again, came to the tomb; it was a cave, and a stone lay upon it.* ³⁹ *Jesus said, "Take away the stone." Martha, the sister of the dead man, said to him, "Lord, by this time there will be an odor, for he has been dead four days."* ⁴⁰ *Jesus said to her, "Did I not tell you that if you would believe you would see the glory of God?"* ⁴¹ *So they took away the stone. And Jesus lifted up his eyes and said, "Father, I thank thee that thou hast heard me.* ⁴² *I knew that thou hearest me always, but I have said this on account of the people standing by, that they may believe that thou didst send me."* ⁴³ *When he had said this, he cried with a loud voice, "Laz'arus, come out."* ⁴⁴ *The dead man came out, his hands and feet bound with bandages, and his face wrapped with a cloth. Jesus said to them, "Unbind him, and let him go."*

⁴⁵ *Many of the Jews therefore, who had come with Mary and had seen what he did, believed in him.*

❧

106

15.

Believe Like Your Life Depended on It

John 11:1-45 RSV

You know what it's like: Someone you love has died. Family and friends come together to grieve. You pay your respects and say your final farewells. And, when you can, you try to put it all in perspective. When a loved one dies, you want answers to life-and-death questions. That's where your beliefs come in. That's *why* we believe: life and death.

A cynical character in an old movie once said, "Everybody dies."[131] He's right, of course. If you haven't died, you will. The Bible says, *"...it is appointed unto men once to die..."*[132]

You're born. You live for a little while. And then you die.

How does that song go?

> "Is that all there is, my friend?
> If that's all there is, my friend,
> then let's keep dancing.
> Let's break out the booze
> and have a ball."

৯৶৶

---

131 John Garfield's character, Charlie Davis, in the movie *Heart and Soul*, 1947.
132 Hebrews 9:27, KJV.

And that's exactly how a lot of people choose to deal with this business of life and death: Act as though you believe death isn't going to happen or, at least, that it doesn't matter.

But it does matter. *"It is appointed unto men once to die—but after this the judgment."* [133] You see, this life, and death, is not all there is—contrary to what the song says. And as it stands, everybody who dies—which means *every*body—dies in trespasses and sin,[134] which is not a good condition to be in if, after death, there is a judgment.

Everybody who dies goes to judgment guilty—unless somebody does something about that not-so-good condition. If somebody can get dead people past the judgment, the Bible says there's a different, better kind of life on the other side.[135]

Well, guess what. Jesus says He can do something about that condition. Jesus says He is the Resurrection and the Life. Jesus says, *"he who believes in me, though he die, yet shall he live, and whoever lives and believes in me shall never die."*

And to prove it, Jesus goes to Bethany, where his dear friend Lazarus has just been buried, not to pay His respects to the dead, but to bring the dead back to life.

Jesus loves Lazarus like a brother, but if you look closely you'll see that Jesus isn't raising Lazarus because He loves him. Jesus has come to the graveyard to reveal the glory of God, so that those who see a dead man living will believe. It's a matter of life and death—and life—for them.

It's the same for us. Our very lives are formed by our beliefs.

What happens when you believe in something—when you are convinced it is real or true?

You organize your world—your reality—based on that belief. You act—or don't act—based on it. Your beliefs determine the meaning of your life and how you will interpret what you experience.

---

[133] Hebrews 9:27, KJV.
[134] Ephesians 2:1.
[135] Revelation 21:1-7.

Do you realize that your beliefs will determine what options will be available to you, at any particular moment, and over time?

The beliefs of each moment position you for, and propel you into, the future. Your beliefs have immediate and long-term consequences.

That's why Jesus was more concerned about everybody's beliefs than about Martha's grief, His disciples' fear, or the misapprehension of the crowds. You've seen the *death* of Lazarus. If you believe, you will see the *glory* of God.

Why believe?

It's a matter of life and death.

❧

Of course, *what* you believe also matters. In the old days, you were told what to believe. You learned your catechism or they glued the church covenant in the back of the hymnals. You accepted what your church taught, or you joined some other church based on their stated beliefs.

Today, it's different. Today, you're free to craft a creed to satisfy personal preference: "I believe Jesus could have done this; I don't believe Jesus could have done that."

Does it matter what we believe?

According to Jesus, it does. Jesus placed more importance on what people believed than on the life of his friend Lazarus—or His own life, for that matter. Jesus raised Lazarus to show his sister Martha and everybody else what they could and should believe in.

Jesus defines what we must believe if we are to see the glory of God revealed—if we are to live. Jesus says, "If you believe in Me, you will live, even though you die. If you believe in Me, even after you die, you will live again and forever."

On the other hand, if you *don't* believe this, it won't happen—can't happen. If you don't believe that Jesus is the Resurrection and the Life, when you die, you die and have to deal with that "judgment thing." There is no "life again"; there is no "eternal life," no "never die."

But this "life after death" and "eternal life" stuff is not easy to believe today. Things are different now. We know things they didn't know back then. We have science and technology.

And does science know all? Is science never wrong about what it claims to know? Has science been to the realm beyond death? Has science measured the immeasurable?

It is easy to say there is nothing beyond the limits of our technology, because if there were something beyond that point, our technology would go there.

I don't believe that at all. There are deep and mysterious realities our hearts and minds sense, in life and beyond, that never show up on the radar screens of modern science.

Jesus says, "If you don't believe I can raise dead people to life again, you won't believe that I can raise you to life again. And if you don't believe I can raise you to life again, I won't. I will only raise those who believe I will. But first, you have to believe I can."

Let me ask you: Are you willing to believe in something you can't control?

You can say, "I don't believe in that." If that's your belief, it will probably *not* be so—for you. But that's a very different thing from: "It can't be so at all, because I don't believe it."

Don't misunderstand: The call of Jesus to believe is not a call to be gullible or naïve. The kind of believing Jesus demands is trusting with your eyes wide open. It is looking clearly, and recognizing the risks involved, and choosing to believe in Jesus Christ when the other options—and there are certainly other options out there—when those other options seem very, very attractive.

Then or now, it is Jesus Who decides what we have to believe. *"I am the resurrection and the life,"* He says. *"He who believes in me, though he die, yet shall he live, and whoever lives and believes in me shall never die. Do you believe this?"*

What you believe is a matter of life and death. Jesus says you need to get this part right. He will not grade this one on the curve.

❧

What we believe is important, but so is *how* we believe.

Believing is not about being holy, or religious in some conventional way. It's not about being good at being good. Believing, as Jesus defines it, is about whether or not you are willing to accept something as true or real—or at least possible.

Are you willing to let God's revelation of reality define the meaning of your life? Are you willing for God to tell you what your life and experiences *mean?*

"I am the resurrection and the life," He says. *"He who believes in me, though he die, yet shall he live, and whoever lives and believes in me shall never die. Do you believe this?"*

"Yes, Lord, I believe," says Martha.

"Then *take away the stone.*"

"WHAT?!"

❧

It's one thing to "like" an idea; it's another to genuinely believe something is so. What we do reveals what we believe—and what we don't believe.

Martha says she believes, but what she does shows that she does not believe Jesus is going to bring Lazarus back to life.

"Do you believe this?"

"Yes, Lord, I believe…"

"Then *take away the stone.*"

"We can't do that, because…well…he's dead in there (and we don't really believe)."

"Roll away the stone."

"But there's no point. It's over. It's too late. He's dead. Things don't work that way."

"Roll the stone away."

"Jesus, I love You and all, and I believe You're the most wonderful thing in the world, but some things just aren't possible."

Jesus gets less argument from Lazarus about coming back from the dead than He does from the man's friends and family about letting him out of the tomb.

If you believe, what are you going to do? What are you going to let God do?

Jesus means to overcome death and restore life and reveal God's glory so people will believe, not just that *"in Adam all die,"* but that *"in Christ shall all be made alive."* [136]

If you believe, roll away the stone. Get the obstacles you've put in God's way out of the way. Roll away the stone from your mind and believe that Jesus is the Power sent from a God Who desires that you live and not die. Roll away the stone from your heart so that death may come out and life may go in.

It's true, Jesus doesn't give you anything easy to believe in. The disciples think, "I believe He's going to get Himself killed—and us, too, probably." And they're right: He does.

And they go with Him anyway, because they've come to believe there's more to this Man Jesus than dying. They believe there's life in this Guy—life now like nothing they've ever experienced, and life after the death He's going to lead them to and through.

"Let's go and die with Him." Thomas wouldn't have said that unless he believed in Jesus more than life itself.

That's believing *what* Jesus wants you to believe. And that's believing *how* Jesus wants you to. *"I am the Resurrection and the Life....though he die, yet shall he live.... If you believe, you will see the glory of God.... Do you believe this?"*

Do *you* believe this?

Take away the stone.

☜❦☞

---

[136] 1 Corinthians 15:22, RSV.

2 Corinthians 5:1-10 ESV

¹ *For we know that if the tent that is our earthly home is destroyed, we have a building from God, a house not made with hands, eternal in the heavens.* ² *For in this tent we groan, longing to put on our heavenly dwelling,* ³ *if indeed by putting it on we may not be found naked.* ⁴ *For while we are still in this tent, we groan, being burdened—not that we would be unclothed, but that we would be further clothed, so that what is mortal may be swallowed up by life.* ⁵ *He who has prepared us for this very thing is God, who has given us the Spirit as a guarantee.*

⁶ *So we are always of good courage. We know that while we are at home in the body we are away from the Lord,* ⁷ *for we walk by faith, not by sight.* ⁸ *Yes, we are of good courage, and we would rather be away from the body and at home with the Lord.* ⁹ *So whether we are at home or away, we make it our aim to please him.* ¹⁰ *For we must all appear before the judgment seat of Christ, so that each one may receive what is due for what he has done in the body, whether good or evil.*

పఈ

John 11:1-45 ESV

¹ *Now a certain man was ill, Lazarus of Bethany, the village of Mary and her sister Martha.* ² *It was Mary who anointed the Lord with ointment and wiped his feet with her hair, whose brother Lazarus was ill.* ³ *So the sisters sent to him, saying, "Lord, he whom you love is ill."* ⁴ *But when Jesus heard it he said, "This illness does not lead to death. It is for the glory of God, so that the Son of God may be glorified through it."*

⁵ *Now Jesus loved Martha and her sister and Lazarus.* ⁶ *So, when he heard that Lazarus was ill, he stayed two days longer in the place where he was.* ⁷ *Then after this he said to the disciples, "Let us go to Judea again."* ⁸ *The disciples said to him, "Rabbi, the Jews were just now seeking to stone you, and are you going there again?"* ⁹ *Jesus answered, "Are there not twelve hours in the day? If anyone walks in the day, he does not stumble, because he sees the light of this world.* ¹⁰ *But if anyone walks in the night, he stumbles, because the light is not in him."* ¹¹ *After saying these things, he said to them, "Our friend Lazarus has fallen asleep, but I go to awaken him."* ¹² *The disciples said to him, "Lord, if he has fallen asleep, he will recover."* ¹³ *Now Jesus had spoken of his death, but they thought that he meant taking rest in sleep.* ¹⁴ *Then Jesus told them plainly, "Lazarus has died,* ¹⁵ *and for your sake I am glad that I was not there, so that you may believe. But let us go to him."* ¹⁶ *So Thomas, called the Twin, said to his fellow disciples, "Let us also go, that we may die with him."*

¹⁷ *Now when Jesus came, he found that Lazarus had already been in the tomb four days.* ¹⁸ *Bethany was near Jerusalem, about two miles off,* ¹⁹ *and many of the Jews had come to Martha and Mary to console them concerning their brother.* ²⁰ *So when Martha heard that Jesus was coming, she went and met him, but Mary remained seated in the house.* ²¹ *Martha said to Jesus, "Lord, if you had been here, my brother would not have died.* ²² *But even now I know that whatever you ask from God, God will give you."* ²³ *Jesus said to her, "Your brother will rise again."* ²⁴ *Martha said to him, "I know that he will rise again in the resurrection on the last day."* ²⁵ *Jesus said to her, "I am the resurrection and the life. Whoever believes in me, though he die, yet shall he live,* ²⁶ *and everyone who lives and believes in me shall never die. Do you believe*

this?" ²⁷ She said to him, "Yes, Lord; I believe that you are the Christ, the Son of God, who is coming into the world."

²⁸ When she had said this, she went and called her sister Mary, saying in private, "The Teacher is here and is calling for you." ²⁹ And when she heard it, she rose quickly and went to him. ³⁰ Now Jesus had not yet come into the village, but was still in the place where Martha had met him. ³¹ When the Jews who were with her in the house, consoling her, saw Mary rise quickly and go out, they followed her, supposing that she was going to the tomb to weep there. ³² Now when Mary came to where Jesus was and saw him, she fell at his feet, saying to him, "Lord, if you had been here, my brother would not have died." ³³ When Jesus saw her weeping, and the Jews who had come with her also weeping, he was deeply moved in his spirit and greatly troubled. ³⁴ And he said, "Where have you laid him?" They said to him, "Lord, come and see." ³⁵ Jesus wept. ³⁶ So the Jews said, "See how he loved him!" ³⁷ But some of them said, "Could not he who opened the eyes of the blind man also have kept this man from dying?"

³⁸ Then Jesus, deeply moved again, came to the tomb. It was a cave, and a stone lay against it. ³⁹ Jesus said, "Take away the stone." Martha, the sister of the dead man, said to him, "Lord, by this time there will be an odor, for he has been dead four days." ⁴⁰ Jesus said to her, "Did I not tell you that if you believed you would see the glory of God?" ⁴¹ So they took away the stone. And Jesus lifted up his eyes and said, "Father, I thank you that you have heard me. ⁴² I knew that you always hear me, but I said this on account of the people standing around, that they may believe that you sent me." ⁴³ When he had said these things, he cried out with a loud voice, "Lazarus, come out." ⁴⁴ The man who had died came out, his hands and feet bound with linen strips, and his face wrapped with a cloth. Jesus said to them, "Unbind him, and let him go."

⁴⁵ Many of the Jews therefore, who had come with Mary and had seen what he did, believed in him.

❧❧

16.

Coming Back

2 Corinthians 5:1-10; John 11:1-45 ESV

Many years ago, I heard a young woman sing a hauntingly beautiful song about heaven. I hear it again from time to time, and every time I do, it has that same beautiful, haunting appeal. It begins like this:

> "They say that heaven's pretty,
> and living here is, too.
> But if they said that I would have
> to choose between the two,
> I'd go home—
> I'd go home—where I belong."[137]

It reminds me a little of what Paul was saying to the Corinthians: "*...we would rather be away from the body and at home with the Lord...to put on our heavenly dwelling...a building from God, a house not made with hands, eternal in the heavens*"

When he wrote that, Paul was not being morbid. It wasn't a "death wish." It was a "life wish," really—an "eternal life wish." It's just a simple comparison—a choosing between two options: Of the two places—here or heaven—where would you rather be?

---

137 Pat Terry, "Home Where I Belong," *Songs of the South*, 1976.

Of course, nobody raises that question in John, Chapter 11, when Jesus raises His dear friend Lazarus from the dead. Word is brought to Jesus that Lazarus is sick—dying, really—because dying was what usually happened when you got sick in that place and time.

And, as it happens, Lazarus lived and died in an especially dangerous place—dangerous for Jesus. Lazarus and his sisters made their home in the little village of Bethany, a suburb of Jerusalem, which was the hub of growing hostility to Jesus. Bethany is only a couple of miles from Jerusalem, about as far as we are, sitting here, from the clubhouse at Whispering Pines or Longleaf.[138]

And so it will take no time at all for word to get back to the big-wigs in the capital that Jesus is back in Judea—down there in Bethany—and for "enemy agents" to come down and see what He is up to. Jesus comes back to Bethany to raise Lazarus from the dead, and by doing so, brings His own death that much closer.[139]

At His command, Lazarus comes back to life, and because of that, Mary and Martha come back to life, in a way—from hopeless, overwhelming grief to all-consuming joy.

☙•❧

All this year, we have been following in the footsteps of Jesus, going where He goes, hearing the good news He preaches, watching the amazing miracles He performs. And no miracle is more amazing than the raising of Lazarus. Jesus puts life back into a decomposing body. He opens the way out of the darkness of the grave into the bright and beautiful light of day. He frees Lazarus from the constraints that bind him and blind him and cut him off from the people who love him.

---

[138] Two of the almost four dozen golf courses in the Pinehurst, North Carolina area, where this sermon was preached.
[139] John 11:53.

It is certainly an amazing miracle, and everybody will be talking about it, whether they're praising God or plotting to do away with Jesus for giving so many people so much to praise God for.

But the one person who isn't talking about what Jesus has done is Lazarus. There's Lazarus, their own local "dead man walking,"[140] and nobody thinks to stick a microphone in his face after they've removed the cloth that was wrapped around it and ask him what somebody would certainly be asking him today:

৯৯

"Lazarus, what was it like to be dead?

"How do you feel right now?

"What are you going to do?

"Have you signed a book deal?

"Have you sold the movie rights?"

Jesus comes and calls into a tomb and Lazarus comes out of that tomb, and as far as everybody watching is concerned, Lazarus has just come back to life.

Hallelujah!

৯৯

But where has Lazarus come back *from?*

Lazarus, we presume, is a man of faith in Jesus—a man, they make a point to say, that Jesus loved. May we presume that when he died, his soul departed his body and went to heaven?

If so, a case could be made for supposing that Jesus did Lazarus no favor by calling him back from heaven—back from God's eternity and all its unimaginable glory—to take up residence once again in a body that, just four days earlier, was dead and done for—to come back to this breathing, eating, waking, sleeping, struggling existence we call "life on earth."

---

140 Movie *Dead Man Walking*, 1995.

You could forgive Lazarus for being not the most grateful guest of honor at the "welcome back" party.

Remember that song about heaven I was telling you about? The second verse goes like this:

> "Sometimes when I'm dreaming,
> it comes as no surprise,
> That if you'll look you'll see
> that homesick feeling in my eyes.
> I'm going home—
> I'm going home—
> where I belong."[141]

It's possible that in their excitement to see Lazarus back from the dead, Mary and Martha and the others might have missed—

"that homesick feeling in [his] eyes."

But Jesus wouldn't have missed it. And He wouldn't have been surprised to see it.

So why do it? Why raise Lazarus from the dead?

Jesus did not call His dear friend back from the greatest, most glorious experience Lazarus had ever known to bless Lazarus. Nor did Jesus raise Lazarus from the dead for Himself, even though it is clear that the death of Lazarus, and the grief that it caused everyone, moved Jesus deeply.

❧

Jesus raised Lazarus for the others—for Mary and Martha, who were beside themselves with sorrow because they thought it was too late for even Jesus to do anything about it, and for all the village women sitting in ashes on their dirt floor mourning with them.

Jesus raised Lazarus for His disciples—for Thomas, who was willing to come to Bethany and die with Jesus, but couldn't imagine the Resurrection of Jesus after He was crucified—and for Simon Peter, who was ready to fight for Jesus before He was arrested, but

---

141 Ibid., p. 117.

couldn't imagine that he would deny Him after—and even for Judas Iscariot, who was already imagining how he would betray Jesus.

And Jesus brought Lazarus back for the spies in the crowd who would skip the celebration so they could hurry back up the hill to Jerusalem to report to the chief priest and his cronies who would decide that Jesus deserves to die for this stunt—and Lazarus, too, for that matter[142]—so that there will be no misunderstanding about where the authority over life and death—or at least death—lies.

The spies and the big-wigs they work for are kind of like those brothers of the rich man in hell that Jesus tells about in the Gospel of Luke—the rich man who, by the way, begs Abraham up in heaven to send Lazarus—a different Lazarus, but a Lazarus who is also enjoying the glory of heaven—back to earth to warn the brothers to repent while they still can.[143]

Just goes to show: Bring a Lazarus back from heaven and there will still be unbelievers!

હ•

Was it worth it? Was it worth it for Jesus to bring His friend Lazarus back from heaven?

What you've got to remember is that the Jesus Who brings Lazarus back from heaven is also the Son of God Who was willing to sacrifice His own place in heaven to come to earth so that all of us who were never going to heaven without His help, could.[144]

And This is the Jesus Who was willing to sacrifice His life on earth—all He had left—for the same reason—even knowing that once He was dead, He wouldn't have the power to get Himself back to heaven and would have to trust His Heavenly Father for that[145]—just as He called on everyone else to do.

---

[142] John 12:10.
[143] Luke 16:19-31.
[144] Philippians 2:5-8.
[145] Luke 23:46.

Jesus wasn't doing Lazarus any favors by bringing him back to life. What Jesus was doing was God's will, as usual. This is the Jesus Who is determined to make that unbelievable possibility—heaven—a little easier to believe, and so He calls Lazarus—His good friend Lazarus—back—for a time—to show them (and us) a preview of "coming heavenly attractions."

And Lazarus sacrifices his place in heaven at his Lord's command. Having gained the glorious prize, Lazarus gives it up again at a word from Jesus, for already, in heaven, every word of Jesus is heard and obeyed, gladly.

And interestingly, the chorus from that song I've been telling you about goes:

> "But while I'm here, I'll serve Him gladly,
> and sing Him all these songs.
> I'm here—but not for long."

⁖∘⁗

Again, it's kind of like Paul in Second Corinthians: *"…we would rather be away from the body and at home with the Lord. So whether we are at home or away, we make it our aim to please him."*

Is Lazarus happy to be back?

I doubt it.

But is he happy to serve the One Who made heaven possible for him in the first place, even if now it means leaving it all behind?

Apparently. Because there he is, bigger than life, or full of *earthly* life, at least—coming out of the grave—the place where life ends, from the world's perspective—but to Lazarus, the place where life everlasting began.

> "But while I'm here, I'll serve Him gladly…
> I'm here, but not for long."

You see, however Lazarus feels about being back in this world—in this life—after tasting the glory of heaven, he can serve the Lord gladly because he knows what heaven is like—and he knows he's going back. The Lazarus who had not died did not know these things—not with the certainty the Lazarus Jesus has brought back from the dead does.

☙❧

And what kind of life do you live if you *know*—beyond a shadow of a doubt—that there *is* a heaven and that it is infinitely greater than anything the human mind can imagine or the human tongue can tell—and that you *are*—beyond a shadow of a doubt—going there to live a life like no life you ever lived before—a life *"eternal in the heavens"* that will never end or fade—that will never frustrate or disappoint or pain you, no matter what, forever?

The last verse of that song about heaven goes:

> "When I'm feeling lonely,
> and when I'm feeling blue,
> It's such a joy to know
> that I am only passing through.
> I'm headed home,
> I'm going home—
> where I belong."

Poor Lazarus, he had to come back from heaven so those he loved—and those he didn't even know, whom God loved—could see that, with Jesus, there is life after death. His coming back was a sign—an amazing, marvelous, miraculous sign—of what is to come for those who come back to God—in repentance and faith and hope.

Lazarus died again, of course, as people do in this world. Even after Jesus brought him back, he was "only passing through." You'll be pleased to know that Lazarus went home again, to heaven, where he belongs.

Are you heading home, where you belong?

You're only passing through this life, you know. But if heaven is your home, you can only get there by coming to the One Who brought Lazarus back from there.

Heaven and earth—you do have to choose between the two, as it turns out, and the sooner the better—'cause like the song says, "[You're] here, but not for long."

Let's head home—where we belong.

৵৶

John 12:1-8 NRSV

¹ Six days before the Passover Jesus came to Bethany, the home of Lazarus, whom he had raised from the dead. ² There they gave a dinner for him. Martha served, and Lazarus was one of those at the table with him. ³ Mary took a pound of costly perfume made of pure nard, anointed Jesus' feet, and wiped them with her hair. The house was filled with the fragrance of the perfume. ⁴ But Judas Iscariot, one of his disciples (the one who was about to betray him), said, ⁵ "Why was this perfume not sold for three hundred denarii and the money given to the poor?" ⁶ (He said this not because he cared about the poor, but because he was a thief; he kept the common purse and used to steal what was put into it.) ⁷ Jesus said, "Leave her alone. She bought it so that she might keep it for the day of my burial. ⁸ You always have the poor with you, but you do not always have me."

ॐॐ

17.

A Dinner in Bethany

John 12:1-8 NRSV

Friday night, we had a special dinner here at The Village Chapel. Chapel Hall was packed and we had a great time. I found myself looking around the room to see who was there. I recognized most people, including some of you. And there were some people I did not know.

We read about another special dinner a moment ago—one held in the village of Bethany on the outskirts of Jerusalem. Let's go to that dinner—and look around the room. Some of the people you won't know, but there are a few there you can't miss.

❧

There is Jesus, of course, the Guest of honor. His friends have invited Him to dinner and He comes, just like He promised in Revelation: *"...if anyone hears my voice and opens the door, I will come in to him and eat with him, and he with me."* [146]

What do you feed the One Who is the Bread of Life? What do you offer the Living Water to drink? Imagine planning the menu for a dinner with Jesus.

---

[146] Revelation 3:20, RSV.

There is Jesus at the head of the table. Next to Him is a fellow named Lazarus. The house belongs to Lazarus and his family, and so Lazarus is the host. Jesus, the special Guest, will sit in the place of honor at his right hand.

Lazarus, as you will recall, had died and Jesus brought him back to life. Now they are sharing a meal together. It's kind of like when every one of us comes to communion: People who were dead, that Jesus brought back to life, now share a meal with Him.

కా

But keep looking.

There's Martha, sister of Lazarus, showing hospitality— serving Jesus and the other guests. She is a good soul; the dinner will not take place without her. God bless her and all like her.

But keep looking.

There are two more people you will recognize. There is Mary, the sister of Martha and Lazarus, and there is Judas Iscariot, who is like a brother to Jesus, and treasurer of the Twelve Jesus has called to be His inner circle of disciples.

కా

For right now, you can ignore everybody else besides Mary and Judas and Jesus. Mary and Judas are each holding something. Judas has a purse that holds the few coins they keep in common. Mary has a parcel that holds enough perfume to blanket the room with a beautiful aroma—enough perfume to fill the purse of Judas with coins if the parcel were sold and the profits provided to him.

But Mary doesn't sell the perfume, she pours it out on the feet of Jesus and soaks up the excess with her hair. Both Jesus and Judas are moved by what Mary has done, but in very different ways.

Judas is calculating—doing the math—condemning an extravagant, excessive sacrifice of love for the One Who brought her brother back from the dead.

Jesus, on the other hand, is confirming the commitment of her valuable gift to Him, understanding that God is consecrating it even as she is giving it.

And here, even Mary fades back into the crowd as Jesus and Judas "discuss" what has been done. And here's a piece of advice: Be careful when Judas is the one who sounds compassionate and Jesus sounds callous.

"The money could have been given to the poor," says Judas.

"The poor you will always have with you," replies Jesus.

৯৯

I'd love to unpack this at length, but time is running out; let's get to the point. Jesus fed the hungry and embraced the poor. But the alleviation of hunger and the elimination of poverty were not the purpose for His presence among us. They were signs of a reality far more significant and far-reaching.

Do not be distracted from your focus on Jesus by all the good and worthy causes in this world that clamor for your attention and your resources. Your commitment to Jesus is more important than any other commitment—even to things you might do in His Name.

In a moment, you will be going to "dinner with Jesus," sharing His table. You were dead, but He brought you back to life.

What valuable thing will you pour out in love for Him?

৯৯

Psalm 92 NRSV

¹ *It is good to give thanks to the* LORD,
  to sing praises to your name, O Most High;
² *to declare your steadfast love in the morning,*
  and your faithfulness by night,
³ *to the music of the lute and the harp,*
  to the melody of the lyre.
⁴ *For you, O* LORD, *have made me glad by your work;*
  at the works of your hands I sing for joy.
⁵ *How great are your works, O* LORD!
  Your thoughts are very deep!
⁶ *The dullard cannot know,*
  the stupid cannot understand this:
⁷ *though the wicked sprout like grass*
  and all evildoers flourish,
they are doomed to destruction forever,
⁸   *but you, O* LORD, *are on high forever.*
⁹ *For your enemies, O* LORD,
  for your enemies shall perish;
  all evildoers shall be scattered.
¹⁰ *But you have exalted my horn like that of the wild ox;*
  you have poured over me fresh oil.
¹¹ *My eyes have seen the downfall of my enemies;*
  my ears have heard the doom of my evil assailants.
¹² *The righteous flourish like the palm tree,*
  and grow like a cedar in Lebanon.
¹³ *They are planted in the house of the* LORD;
  they flourish in the courts of our God.
¹⁴ *In old age they still produce fruit;*
  they are always green and full of sap,
¹⁵ *showing that the* LORD *is upright;*
  he is my rock, and there is no unrighteousness in him.

෴

John 15:1-8 NRSV

[Jesus said:]

^{1} *"I am the true vine, and my Father is the vinegrower.* ^{2} *He removes every branch in me that bears no fruit. Every branch that bears fruit he prunes to make it bear more fruit.* ^{3} *You have already been cleansed by the word that I have spoken to you.* ^{4} *Abide in me as I abide in you. Just as the branch cannot bear fruit by itself unless it abides in the vine, neither can you unless you abide in me.* ^{5} *I am the vine, you are the branches. Those who abide in me and I in them bear much fruit, because apart from me you can do nothing.* ^{6} *Whoever does not abide in me is thrown away like a branch and withers; such branches are gathered, thrown into the fire, and burned.* ^{7} *If you abide in me, and my words abide in you, ask for whatever you wish, and it will be done for you.* ^{8} *My Father is glorified by this, that you bear much fruit and become my disciples."*

∽✑

18.

Bearing Fruit

Psalm 92; John 15:1-8 NRSV

Today is Mothers' Day.

I mention this fact at the beginning of the sermon because it may have slipped the attention of someone among us and, if so, you will want to remedy that oversight while there is still time, technically, to do so.

I will warn you, the cards will be pretty well picked over by now, but that may be the least of your problems if you have not wished the appropriate person "Happy Mothers' Day" by now.

We honor and celebrate our mothers, you who are here and those who are elsewhere, mothers living and those who have departed this life. Our presence on this earth is proof that our mothers have borne fruit, in the biological sense, as when the mother of John the Baptist said to the Virgin Mary, *"Blessed is the fruit of your womb."*

But mothers have borne fruit in other ways as well, in our lives and in the lives of others. It would be an emotional and extended service if we were to dwell on the fruit our mothers have borne in most of us from the day of our birth even until now. Their impact surely continues and for their positive contributions to our lives, we give God thanks.

The Bible addresses this business of bearing fruit today, both in the Gospel we heard and in the Psalter we read together. In the Psalter, God's people are likened to flourishing palm and cedar trees, figuratively "planted" in the House of God. The image "works" because these godly people are frequently in the temple physically and constantly focused on the God of that temple spiritually. As a result, they will still bear fruit (spiritually) in old age, and stay fresh and green with a spiritual vigor more common to "plants" in their physical prime.

In the Gospel of John, Jesus picks up the fruit-bearing metaphor as He prepares His disciples for His death. The image Jesus uses is even more familiar to those raised on the sacred writings of Israel than the trees of Psalm 92. From the Prophet Hosea[147] to Isaiah[148] to Jeremiah[149] to Ezekiel,[150] Israel as a people and as a nation had been represented throughout the centuries as a vine that God had planted and tended. But the prophets consistently condemned Israel for not bearing the fruit it should have, given God's care and attention.

And now, as the final dark hours pass before Jesus is arrested, He tells His disciples that He, not Israel, is the true Vine that God has planted. He is the Vine—and they are the branches—branches that, if firmly attached to the Vine, will bear much fruit.

❧

But here's where it gets tricky. Here's one of those places where you need to study the Bible and not just read it, because if you're not careful, you'll just hear what you think it says—what you expect it to say. Jesus says, *"I am the vine, you are the branches. Those who abide in me…bear much fruit."*

---

147 Hosea 10:1.
148 Isaiah 5:7.
149 Jeremiah 2:4, 21.
150 Ezekiel 15.

Please note that Jesus is not telling His disciples to bear much fruit. Nowhere in this passage does Jesus say, "Come on, guys, bear more fruit."

What He does say to them—and to us—is, *"Abide in me—remain with Me."* If you do so, you will bear much fruit. And this is the *only* way you will be able to bear much fruit. But more important even than bearing fruit is abiding in Jesus.

Yes, God's goal is that we bear fruit, but this is not a pep rally or some high-pressure sales meeting pushing the staff to work harder and close more deals. God knows you can't do on your own what God's chosen people never could before the coming of Jesus. You can't bear fruit—the kind of fruit God wants to see—if you are not a part of Jesus—if you are not drawing your spiritual life support directly and completely from Him. Whatever you're doing, you will not bear the fruit God desires if you are not so completely attached to His Vine, to Jesus, that all the power involved in bearing fruit comes from Him and Him alone.

It is true that if you are not a branch connected to the true Vine, you still may be able to accomplish any number of wonderful and impressive things as a result of the determined application of your own energy, intellect, personal resources and interests. But as far as God is concerned, you are not bearing the fruit *He* desires—you are bearing *your* fruit, not His.

And if you are not bearing the fruit God desires (and that He is pruning and getting rid of branches to achieve), you can guess what God will do with you. God prunes, or He removes branches entirely and destroys them. Take your pick.

But realize that even when you give up trying to bear fruit for God through your own initiative—even when you let the true Vine nurture and nourish everything in you, God will still shape and mold you so that you continually close in on your God-given fruit-bearing potential.

അ‑ഌ

And then there's this: Jesus says, *"…apart from me, you can do nothing."*

Sometimes, we get going so fast mentally that we tend to miss the significance of something—or miss that something is significant to begin with. It's like barreling down the road so fast you miss the speed limit sign or the detour notice. This can easily be one of those times, so as the fellow says, "Here's your sign."

"Apart from me, you can do nothing." You can be busy in acts of service—you can be immersed in honorable pursuits. But in God's eyes, you are spinning your spiritual wheels. You're a branch lying around in God's vineyard hoping—perhaps even believing—there is some other way to bear fruit than by being closely attached to the Vine.

But there isn't. *"Abide in me as I abide in you… The branch cannot bear fruit by itself; it must abide in the vine. Those who abide in me and I in them bear much fruit."*

Do you hear it?

Abide. That's what Jesus is talking about. That's what Jesus is so concerned that His disciples hear.

Abide: Devote yourself to being with Jesus, mentally, spiritually, emotionally, physically. Wake up with Him in the morning and spend the day with Him and close your eyes in sleep at the end of your day with Jesus as your final thought. And then do the exact same thing the next day, and the next, and every day. Do not be satisfied paying Jesus a hurried visit, or offering Him a fleeting prayer. Do not treat Him like a *twitter* friend.

Abide in Him. Move away from the margins of relationship with Jesus and navigate to the center of His presence with you.

Abide in Jesus by abiding in His Word. Look for His wisdom, His comfort, His encouragement, His guidance and nurture in what He has said and what He has done, as recorded in Scripture. Realize that "beyond the sacred page,"[151] as the hymn describes it,

---

[151] Mary A. Lathbury, "Break Thou the Bread of Life," 1877.

is the Holy Spirit, waiting to reveal to you the mind of Jesus on whatever crisis or concern you face. As the Word of God molds your thinking, it will meld your desires with His divine will. And you will come to pray with the wisdom and power of an "insider" with God.

৵৹৹

What is the result of abiding in Jesus?

Jesus abides in you—and bears God's fruit through you. There is no doubt that Jesus will abide in you, if allowed to do so. The true Vine will do what a vine does if the vine is allowed to: It will nourish its branches and cause its branches to bear fruit, as intended.

Focus on the fruit, and you will fail, no matter how much fruit you want to bear for Jesus. But focus on the relationship with Jesus—abide in Jesus—attach yourself to Him like the branch that extends naturally from a vine, and He will bear fruit through you. The vine will cause the branch that is firmly attached and properly pruned to bear all the fruit that branch is designed and expected to bear.

The relationship is not the end result, of course. We were designed to bear fruit. That is the purpose for our existence. But we will not fulfill that purpose—we will not bear the fruit God desires—until we embrace the relationship in which, and through which, Jesus bears the fruit God desires and designed us to bear.

Do you want to bear fruit, spiritual fruit for eternity?

Abide in the true Vine, Jesus, Who will, in turn, abide in you—always.

৵৹৹

1 John 4:7-11 ESV

^{7} *Beloved, let us love one another, for love is from God, and whoever loves has been born of God and knows God.* ^{8} *Anyone who does not love does not know God, because God is love.* ^{9} *In this the love of God was made manifest among us, that God sent his only Son into the world, so that we might live through him.* ^{10} *In this is love, not that we have loved God but that he loved us and sent his Son to be the propitiation for our sins.* ^{11} *Beloved, if God so loved us, we also ought to love one another.*

৯৩

John 15:9-12 ESV

[Jesus said:]
^{9} *"As the Father has loved me, so have I loved you. Abide in my love.* ^{10} *If you keep my commandments, you will abide in my love, just as I have kept my Father's commandments and abide in his love.* ^{11} *These things I have spoken to you, that my joy may be in you, and that your joy may be full.*

^{12} *"This is my commandment, that you love one another as I have loved you."*

৯৩

19.

And In Conclusion...[152]

1 John 4:7-11; John 15:9-12 ESV

Today is a very special Sunday for us. It is the first anniversary of our moving our Daybreak and Cornerstone worship services from the shadows, the squatty seats and the sloping floors of the theatre at The O'Neal School to this bright, beautiful and well-balanced sanctuary. Today is the first anniversary of the establishment of our NewSong service. And today is the day that the man God has chosen, and you have called, to be Trinity's new Senior Pastor assumes his sacred responsibilities in that role.

Today is a special day for Trinity to celebrate God's remarkable providence in the past and His equally impressive provision for the future. The honors and affection this congregation showered upon me in recent weeks—and especially last Sunday—far exceed what I deserve and do you great honor, and so today may be devoted to looking ahead.

And the best thing I can do to help you get ready for the future you and your new pastor are getting ready to experience is to recall for you what our Lord said to His closest friends and followers in

---

[152] This was the final sermon I preached before retiring as pastor of a church I helped start. At the end of the sermon, I turned over my pastoral responsibilities to my successor who served that day as the worship leader.

His final moments with them—when they were gathered for a final communion together. Jesus said: *"This is my commandment—that you love one another as I have loved you."* Of all the things I could say to you—of all the things Jesus could and did say to you—nothing is more important for you to hear—as individual Christians and as a congregation—than this.

Why is *this* the most important thing I can tell you in my last sermon?

Because it is a commandment from Jesus for His followers—and because, according to 1st John, if you keep this commandment, you have been born of God and know God.

ം

Do you hear what he's saying?

When the people in a congregation do not love one another as Jesus loves them, they are not a church.

Loving one another like Jesus loves you is the one, unassailable proof—to you and to the world—that you are, in fact, a genuine church. It's not the legal paperwork—not impressive architecture—not huge crowds or hefty budgets—not dazzling worship services or diversified ministries—not long tradition on the one hand or up-to-date trendiness on the other.

No matter what else was going on, when we as Trinity have loved one another as Jesus loved us, we have been "quite a church." When we have *not* loved one another—for whatever reason—we have been "not quite a church."

As you go forward, there will likely be disagreements about things theological and practical. We've certainly had our share in the past.

You all will disagree on stuff in the future. All churches do. And you're interdenominational; you were *designed* to!

You will probably get your feelings hurt some time. You may find that your personality just doesn't "mesh" with somebody else's.

When that happens, here's the question: Will you love one another as Jesus loves you—*before* you disagree—and *as* you disagree—and *after* you disagree and, especially, *because* you disagree? Will you make loving one another as Christ has loved you more important—to you and to this church—than being "right," or getting your way, or not being (or staying) hurt or offended?

Before you answer, remember—you are *commanded* to love one another—not by me or by the man who becomes your new pastor today—but by Jesus Himself. And Jesus is not talking about some sappy, sentimental love. He's talking about *His* kind of love—the "I'll climb up on a Cross and suffer and die for the very people who think I'm all wrong, and always oppose Me, and attack Me every time I turn around" kind of love.

Jesus doesn't love us—any of us—because "we're just so *wonderful* how could anybody *not* love us!"

Jesus loves us because we need His love so desperately.

The Bible never says Jesus was just "charmed off His feet" by anyone. It does say—repeatedly—that He had compassion on people because they were so pathetic.

"But…while we were yet sinners Christ died for us."[153]

"Christ loved us and gave himself up for us, a fragrant offering and sacrifice to God."[154]

"Beloved, if God so loved us, we also ought to love one another."

In fact, we're commanded to—by the Son of the God Who (the Bible says) *is* love.

ॐॐ

The love that makes a group of people a genuine church is what 1ˢᵗ John is talking about when he says that *"God is love."* It is not your love—it is God's love—that makes you a church. We did not become a church because we decided to act lovingly toward each other—or even toward God. It was God Who loved us, and

---

[153] Romans 5:8, RSV.
[154] Ephesians 5:2, RSV.

we became aware of that love, and we accepted it, and put our faith in it and became something essentially different because of that love in us, which also enables us to know God in ways we did not know Him before we accepted His love, which makes this remarkable relationship we now have with God possible—individually and collectively—which makes this a church—His church—the church of the God Who is love.

❧

Loving one another is the way God has provided for showing God that you love Him. God doesn't believe any other demonstration of love for Him.

And loving one another is one way—perhaps the most powerful way—God expresses His love to us.

When you are not loving one another, God's love for every one of you is not getting through in the way He intends for it to. God is displeased and the fellowship suffers the "spiritual malnutrition" that always results when the conduit of God's nourishing love is cut off before it reaches its destination.

There is nothing that you can do for this church that will be more beneficial for the future of this church than to love one another as Christ has loved you. There is nothing you can do that will make your new pastor's ministry more God-revealing and God-blessed than to love him and his wife in the same way that Christ has loved you. And there is nothing you can do to bring me more joy in the future as I remember you and love you and pray for you than that each one of you make loving one another—especially when you are inclined not to—the most important thing you do.

Beloved, let us love one another—always.

❧

20.

Cramming for Finals

John 15:9-17 NRSV

[Jesus said:]

⁹ *"As the Father has loved me, so I have loved you; abide in my love.* ¹⁰ *If you keep my commandments, you will abide in my love, just as I have kept my Father's commandments and abide in his love.* ¹¹ *I have said these things to you so that my joy may be in you, and that your joy may be complete.*

¹² *"This is my commandment, that you love one another as I have loved you.* ¹³ *No one has greater love than this, to lay down one's life for one's friends.* ¹⁴ *You are my friends if you do what I command you.* ¹⁵ *I do not call you servants any longer, because the servant does not know what the master is doing; but I have called you friends, because I have made known to you everything that I have heard from my Father.* ¹⁶ *You did not choose me but I chose you. And I appointed you to go and bear fruit, fruit that will last, so that the Father will give you whatever you ask him in my name.* ¹⁷ *I am giving you these commands so that you may love one another."*

❧◦❦

There wasn't much time left and Jesus had to prepare His disciples. Within hours—or minutes—Jesus would be arrested and would never again have an opportunity to tell His disciples anything. And so Jesus was determined to focus on the key points in the little time—the last of the time—He had left with them. Look what He told them—and us—in the verses we just heard. I'll rearrange the order a bit so we can appreciate the significance of what Jesus said.

He began by telling them, *"I have loved you as the Father has loved me."* Imagine going to the store and finding a card that says, "I love you as much as the God of infinite love is capable of loving"? That's what Jesus is saying to His disciples.

Jesus is the Son of God. It is inconceivable that His Heavenly Father would love Jesus any less than the absolute maximum possible for God to love. "And that," Jesus tells His disciples, "is how much I have loved you."

And how is that love demonstrated?

John 3 says, *"The Father loves the Son and has placed everything in his hands."*[155] John 5 says, *"the Father loves the Son and shows him all he does."*[156]

Having clarified for them how much and in what ways He has loved them, Jesus then says to them, "I command you to love one another as I have loved you." He doesn't request, or suggest, or encourage. He commands. "Love one another—love My other disciples—not as they deserve—not as you feel like—but as I love you (which, as you recall, Jesus just defined as the way God loves Him). Love them as much as, and in the same way as, I love you."

That's a tall order. But it's still an order.

And Jesus is not done. Jesus tells them, "I have called you friends, not servants." They are not worthy to even be servants, much less friends. But friends it is—friends to whom Jesus has made known all that He has heard from the Father.

Let that sink in for a minute.

Jesus has called (and therefore, made) His disciples "friends," with all the rights, privileges and blessings pertaining thereunto, both throughout this life and for all eternity.

---

[155] John 3:35, NIV.
[156] John 5:20, NIV.

The disciples of Jesus are not pawns in the cosmic confrontation between good and evil—they are players. They are teammates of Jesus, trusted allies in the campaign to destroy sin and redeem Creation.

In the military, each person is assigned a security clearance that determines what information that individual is allowed to know. In the "army" of Christ, His disciples—His friends—are "cleared" for everything. They have full access. Jesus has made known all that He has heard from the Father.

Did you hear that?

All that Jesus has heard from the Father—all—Jesus has made known to His disciples. And apparently, it's all still there, in the pages of His sacred Word.

These are wonderful promises—amazing gifts. But even with that, Jesus retains the initiative. Before anyone could choose to be a disciple of Jesus, Jesus chose to make it possible. In that way, Jesus claimed the initiative, and maintains it, even now.

He chose His disciples and appointed them to go and bear lasting fruit so that the Father would give them whatever they ask the Father for in Jesus' name.

And here's an odd thing.

On the dark night of what seems to all the disciples like the brink—and then the reality—of complete disaster, Jesus assures them that the reason He has been pumping so much information into their ears is this: joy.

"I have spoken these things to you that my joy may be in you and your joy may be full. Despite the arrest, despite the suffering, despite the Cross (Jesus says)—if you hear what I am telling you—and trust what I am telling you—and do what I am telling you—you will trade fear and sorrow for shear and absolute joy."

And, eventually, that is exactly what those disciples did—and what we do—if we are to be His disciples, too.

൦~൭

Romans 5:6-8 ESV

The Book of Romans is Paul's explanation of man's need—and God's gift—of salvation. In today's reading, Paul sums up what the Crucifixion means for us.

ॐ

⁶ *For while we were still weak, at the right time Christ died for the ungodly.* ⁷ *For one will scarcely die for a righteous person—though perhaps for a good person one would dare even to die—* ⁸ *but God shows his love for us in that while we were still sinners, Christ died for us.*

ॐ

John 15:12-17 ESV

On their last night together, Jesus promoted His followers from servants to friends and commanded them to love one another, defining "love" as the kind of sacrifice He would soon make for them. He also clarified the purpose for which He had chosen them: to go and bear lasting fruit.

ॐ

[Jesus said:]
¹² *"This is my commandment, that you love one another as I have loved you.* ¹³ *Greater love has no one than this, that someone lay down his life for his friends.* ¹⁴ *You are my friends if you do what I command you.* ¹⁵ *No longer do I call you servants, for the servant does not know what his master is doing; but I have called you friends, for all that I have heard from my Father I have made known to you.* ¹⁶ *You did not choose me, but I chose you and appointed you that you should go and bear fruit and that your fruit should abide, so that whatever you ask the Father in my name, he may give it to you.* ¹⁷ *These things I command you, so that you will love one another."*

ॐ

21.

To Love Like Jesus

Romans 5:6-8; John 15:12-17 ESV

It was 50 years ago this year that my father's mother got sick and died with cancer. In the last months of her life, we took her into our home and my mother cared for her. Hospice in those days was a family affair.

Momma Hill was beloved—*revered*, really—by her six surviving children, of whom my father was the eldest. The youngest, my Aunt Virginia, told me years later that in Momma Hill's final days, in her pain and delirium, she would clutch Virginia's hand and plead, "Will you die for me?"

And crushed by her mother's suffering, all Virginia could say was, "Momma, if I could, I would!"

And I suspect she was telling her mother the truth.

৵৽

Across this country and around the world lie multitudes of men and women who died for you and me—in the abstract, at least. Many, no doubt, in the heat of battle, died for someone in particular, the soldier or Marine in the mud beside them—a shipmate at sea or crewmember in the air—the comrade in arms who had, in the crucible of war, become closer than a brother. That is a special kind of love.

It is the greatest kind of love, according to Jesus. To die for someone else—and more specifically, to lay down your life for someone—freely, voluntarily, sacrificially—is perhaps the noblest and most virtuous act a person can perform, which is why we view the graves at Arlington and Gettysburg and Flanders Fields and a hundred other places as hallowed ground.

When asked, "Will you die for me?" they answered, "Yes!"

This weekend we honor the memories of those who died for their country—for the cause of freedom—and for their friends. And today, we use this duty to pay tribute as a springboard to see an even greater example of the greatest kind of love—the love of Jesus for His disciples, His servants, His friends.

My Aunt Virginia wanted to take her mother's place and die for her because my grandmother had spent her life in sacrificial devotion to her children. The warriors who "took a bullet" for their buddies knew their buddies would have—and in many cases had—taken bullets for them.

But, as the Apostle Paul pointed out, *"Christ died for the ungodly…. While we were still sinners, Christ died for us."* Jesus laid down His life for 12 men—and the whole world—not because they or we had earned the favor and deserved the consideration, but because we had *not,* and could not. We had not poured a lifetime of selfless mother-love into Jesus or shared the hardships and hazards of warfare with Him. We were the enemy across the no-man's-land fighting off His every advance. We were the wayward and rebellious children breaking our Heavenly Father's heart at every turn.

Those who died in the service of our country believed they were fighting—and dying—for something worth the sacrifice. God sent Jesus to be the Christ Who would lay down His life for a human race God knew to be completely unworthy of His sacrificial love. God sent Jesus to lay down His life *because* we are unworthy. "We are not worthy so much as to gather up the crumbs under [His] Table"—as the prayer goes[157]—but still Jesus came. And still He called us His friends. And still He laid down His life for His friends—for us.

Jesus laid down His life for us—and so we live. We have "dodged the (divine) bullet"—or the demonic one, depending on your perspective. But either way, *"When you were dead in your sins,"* wrote Paul, *"God made you alive with Christ."*[158]

"Thank you, Jesus! And so long till next time!"

ॐ

But it's not as simple as that. Jesus laid down His life for us—He died for us. Now, having died for us—the unfriendly folks He called "friends"—He commands us to be friends like Him—to love like Him—to lay down our lives like Him.

The command is simple—and repeated for clarity and emphasis.

"God so loved the world..."[159] and so should we, but we start by loving each other. Each of the 12 apostles was commanded to love the 11 other men. Each of us is commanded to love the several hundred other people in this church.

"Love them? I don't even *know* some of them!"

Jesus said, *"Love each other as I have loved you."* Maybe you should spend a little time with the pictorial directory this afternoon and think about how you can love those people in the pictures the way Jesus loves you.

Have you considered that your Savior has commanded you to love the people in the book and in the seats around you like He loves you? And have you considered what that means?

---

[157] From "The Prayer of Humble Confession," The Episcopal *Book of Common Prayer*, 1928. (This was the Order of Service we used in the liturgical communion services each Sunday in the two interdenominational churches I served in Pinehurst, North Carolina.)

[158] Colossians 2:13, NIV.

[159] John 3:16, KJV.

You know what you *think* that means.

Do you know what *Jesus* thinks that means? Do you think you're thinking the same thing as Jesus? What did He want His love to accomplish in your life? What does He want His love in you to accomplish in the lives of others—those He has commanded you to love as He has loved you?

Jesus isn't talking about loving the people you love. He's talking about loving each other—the other people who just happen to be the membership of this little mob of Christians that makes up our church.

"*Love* 'um? I don't even *like* some of them!"

And maybe Jesus didn't like some of the disciples. The Bible doesn't tell us that He liked them. It does tell us He got mad at them—He got frustrated and exasperated with them. He rebuked them,[160] corrected them,[161] challenged them,[162] instructed them[163]—repeatedly, and at great lengths. He intervened in their squabbles.[164] He predicted their denial and desertions, accepted one's betrayal[165]—and died for them—laying down His wonderful, sinless, miracle-working divine-human life for them.

Jesus chose to love them (and us) because that's what God sent Him and commanded Him to do—however He happened to feel about us—however our individual and collective personalities happened to strike Him. Jesus didn't have to like me or my behavior or my attitude or my politics or anything else about me to love me and lay down His life for me.

For that matter, He didn't have to love me and choose me as His friend to die for—except that His Heavenly Father commanded Him to—just as He has commanded me to love you and lay down my life for you. Jesus didn't have to…

---

160 Matthew 8:26; 16:23; Mark 10:13-14; John 14:9.
161 Matthew 18:21-22.
162 Matthew 17:14-20.
163 Mark 4:10-12.
164 Mark 10:35-45.
165 Matthew 26:31; John 13:27.

…except that He *did* have to, if I was going to be "died for," as I had to be, if I wasn't going to have to die for myself, lost and condemned in my sin. Only He could do what had to be done for me—and He did, by loving me enough—for God knows why—to lay down His life for me—and for you.

৯৽৻

What do you do when someone has laid down his life for you?

That's the question they finally come to at the end of the movie *Saving Private Ryan*,[166] which will certainly be on TV somewhere this weekend. One soldier is chosen at the highest level to be saved from the horrors of war and others are ordered to seek him and save him—a stranger—even if they must lay down their own lives to do so—which, in the end, they all do.

What do you do? What do you do when someone has died for you?

That's what Private Ryan asks as he kneels before the cross of the man who accomplished his rescue—the man who died to ensure that he would live.

The best answer the film makers could come up with was: Live a good life—be a good person.

Jesus has a better answer—perhaps because the life He laid down for His friends was a greater, purer, nobler sacrifice than even the one depicted in the movie.

What do you do when this particular Someone has died for you?

You spend the rest of your life loving others as you have been loved by your Savior, laying down your life each day in a love like Jesus loved you with—going and bearing fruit—planting and cultivating in others that same lay-down-your-life love that Jesus—and His friends—have laid down in their lives for you.

৯৽৻

---

[166] Movie *Saving Private Ryan*, 1998.

John 15:26-27; 16:4b-15 NRSV

[Jesus said:]

15 ²⁶ *"When the Advocate comes, whom I will send to you from the Father, the Spirit of truth who comes from the Father, he will testify on my behalf.* ²⁷ *You also are to testify because you have been with me from the beginning."*

16 ⁴ *"...I did not say these things to you from the beginning, because I was with you.* ⁵ *But now I am going to him who sent me; yet none of you asks me, 'Where are you going?'* ⁶ *But because I have said these things to you, sorrow has filled your hearts.* ⁷ *Nevertheless I tell you the truth: it is to your advantage that I go away, for if I do not go away, the Advocate will not come to you; but if I go, I will send him to you.* ⁸ *And when he comes, he will prove the world wrong about sin and righteousness and judgment:* ⁹ *about sin, because they do not believe in me;* ¹⁰ *about righteousness, because I am going to the Father and you will see me no longer;* ¹¹ *about judgment, because the ruler of this world has been condemned.*

¹² *"I still have many things to say to you, but you cannot bear them now.* ¹³ *When the Spirit of truth comes, he will guide you into all the truth; for he will not speak on his own, but will speak whatever he hears, and he will declare to you the things that are to come.* ¹⁴ *He will glorify me, because he will take what is mine and declare it to you.* ¹⁵ *All that the Father has is mine. For this reason I said that he will take what is mine and declare it to you."*

ৡৡ

22.

When the Spirit Comes

John 15:26-27; 16:4b-15 NRSV

I have a friend who, when he comes to visit, will not be satisfied to just sit around and "visit." When he comes, he does things—he takes on projects—he transforms the place.

Jesus tells His disciples as the time of His Crucifixion approaches that He will soon go to be with God the Father in heaven. He promises to send them a divine Helper to take His place. He's talking about the Holy Spirit, but Jesus gives Him different names: Helper, Advocate, Spirit of Truth, Counselor, Paraclete, Comforter.

Whatever He's called, the Holy Spirit is like my friend—at least in this: When the Holy Spirit comes, He will not be content to sit around with us and visit. The Holy Spirit comes to do things. He comes to work.

And Jesus gives a pretty good summary of the Holy Spirit's "To-Do" list in the Gospel reading we just heard. In case you missed it—and you might have, given that it was interwoven in the other things Jesus had to say—let me give it to you again.

Jesus says, *"When the Advocate comes...he will testify on my behalf."* Other translations say, *"He will bear witness to me."*[167]

The earthly ministry of Jesus is coming to an end. Jesus is going away. But the Holy Spirit will come to take His place as the constant Companion, Teacher and Leader of these followers.

The Holy Spirit is sent primarily to the disciples of Jesus, and so the testimony He gives about Jesus will be directed to them. Jesus' disciples will testify to the world about Jesus, but only after the Holy Spirit has testified about Him to them. That you and I today are able to know anything about Jesus—or, in fact, to know Him at all—is the result of the Holy Spirit testifying about Him to them—and to us.

☙

The next item on the Spirit's "To-Do" list is: to *"prove the world wrong"* about right and wrong and where Jesus fits into all that. Jesus says that when the Holy Spirit comes, *"He will convict* (or expose) *the world concerning sin and righteousness and judgment."* [168]

The world decided that Jesus was a sinner and executed Him to prove it. But the Holy Spirit will show that killing Jesus was the sin.[169] The world thought it a good and godly act to kill Jesus, but the Spirit will make sure people know that God raised Jesus from the dead[170] and exalted Him to the highest place in heaven[171] (which God would definitely not do if killing Jesus was as good an idea as the world thought it was).

And the Spirit will show that the crucifixion of Jesus was not a victory by His enemies over Him, but God's victory over them[172]—and God's judgment upon them,[173] if they do not repent.

---

[167] John 15:26, RSV.
[168] John 16:8, ESV.
[169] Acts 2:23.
[170] Acts 3:13-15.
[171] Acts 5:30-32.
[172] 1 Corinthians 15:57.
[173] 2 Corinthians 5:10.

And then Jesus says, *"When the Spirit of truth comes, He will guide you in all the truth…he will declare to you the things that are to come. He will glorify me because he will take what is mine and declare it to you."*

The Holy Spirit will make sense of past, present, and future. He will show you how things really are and what they really mean. He will not leave you vulnerable to the persuasive deceptions of the day.

The first followers of Jesus were very impressed with Jesus—that's why they followed Him in the first place. But the Holy Spirit points out spiritual insights about Jesus the disciples never even considered—and takes them from impressed to awestruck and beyond.

৵◦৻

Don't expect the Holy Spirit to be the divine Friend Who comes to visit with no purpose in mind. When the Holy Spirit comes, He comes to do something important. He comes to take on projects like transforming your life with the powerful knowledge of the Person and significance of Jesus Christ. The Holy Spirit comes to testify to you and through you to the world God is determined to redeem.

It's all right there on His Holy Spirit "To-do" list.

৵◦৻

John 17:6-19 NRSV

[Jesus prayed:]

⁶ *"I have made your name known to those whom you gave me from the world. They were yours, and you gave them to me, and they have kept your word. ⁷ Now they know that everything you have given me is from you; ⁸ for the words that you gave to me I have given to them, and they have received them and know in truth that I came from you; and they have believed that you sent me. ⁹ I am asking on their behalf; I am not asking on behalf of the world, but on behalf of those whom you gave me, because they are yours. ¹⁰ All mine are yours, and yours are mine; and I have been glorified in them. ¹¹ And now I am no longer in the world, but they are in the world, and I am coming to you. Holy Father, protect them in your name that you have given me, so that they may be one, as we are one. ¹² While I was with them, I protected them in your name that you have given me. I guarded them, and not one of them was lost except the one destined to be lost, so that the scripture might be fulfilled. ¹³ But now I am coming to you, and I speak these things in the world so that they may have my joy made complete in themselves. ¹⁴ I have given them your word, and the world has hated them because they do not belong to the world, just as I do not belong to the world. ¹⁵ I am not asking you to take them out of the world, but I ask you to protect them from the evil one. ¹⁶ They do not belong to the world, just as I do not belong to the world. ¹⁷ Sanctify them in the truth; your word is truth. ¹⁸ As you have sent me into the world, so I have sent them into the world. ¹⁹ And for their sakes I sanctify myself, so that they also may be sanctified in truth."*

⊰•⊱

23.

Sent and Sanctified

John 17:6-19 NRSV

The world is at war.

Many of you here, as we saw earlier,[174] have participated in the world's wars. You understand something of war from personal experience. We gather today on the eve of a day devoted to the remembrance of those, known and unknown, who not only served, but sacrificed all, in the cause of freedom and liberty and human value and self-government. The world is still at war, and a new generation takes up the cause and the sacrifice that was ours to make in our youth.

The wars in this world are about territory and ideology, economics and power. The wars we think about first are the wars between nations, but the world is also full of wars between smaller groups, rich and poor, labor and management, liberal and conservative.

The world is a place where families are at war with their neighbors and among themselves: children against parents, husbands against wives and siblings against each other. Individuals

---

[174] This sermon was preached on the Sunday of a Memorial Day weekend. Prior to that service each year, a slide show of pictures of current and deceased church members from their time in the military was presented.

are at war with themselves, struggling with "the person" inside. In reality, the whole world is at war. In each and every case, ultimately, the world is at war with God.

The "world"—when the Bible talks about it—as Jesus talks about it—and prays about it in John 17—is not the world of nature, created and sustained by a loving and gracious God. In John 17, as Jesus lifts His prayers to God, the "world" stands for human society organizing itself without—and, therefore, against— God.

And God, the rightful Sovereign of the world, is unwilling to grant humanity its independence from His divine authority. It cannot survive independent of His divine provision. And so there is war—between a world of humanity that will not be obedient to God on one side, and a God Who will not submit to the world's rebellious agenda on the other. What we have heard in John 17, and what we remember on the eve of Memorial Day, must be considered in this context.

In Chapter 18, Jesus will go to the Garden of Gethsemane where Judas will betray Him to those who will arrest Him and begin the process that will lead to the Cross. But here in John 17, Jesus has gathered His disciples—His troops—around Him on the eve of these events—on the eve of the great battle with the world.

There has been rigorous training and detailed preparation— months of it. Jesus and His men—His unimpressive little squad of men—have made contact with the enemy and fought a few minor skirmishes. But tomorrow will be different. Everything rests on tomorrow. It is to be the battle that will decide who wins the war. It will not be the end of the war, but it will ensure that the war will end, and how it will end.

Jesus has removed His troops from their normal surroundings and routine to focus on their final instructions and equipment issue. And when all that is concluded, Jesus does what many a great warrior will do before a great battle: He prays. When all Jesus needs to say to His disciples has been said, and they remain there gathered close around Him, He lifts His face to heaven and prays. He prays for Himself and He prays for those gathered around Him and He prays for all those who will ultimately come over to His side—who will join His army and serve under His banner.

Jesus prays for them—and for us—because the great battle— the greatest and most consequential battle of all time—is about to begin. And Jesus will fight it alone.[175] There will be other battles— scary, difficult fights—in which these disciples will see action.[176] That's what Jesus has been training them for.

But Jesus is about to take on the whole wicked world—and the evil power that rules it—alone, because Jesus is the only One capable of winning this battle—and because He was sent by His heavenly Father specifically to fight this battle[177]—and because He has dedicated Himself—His whole life and being—to fighting and winning this greatest of all battles.[178]

The battle will cost Him His life—He knows this going in.[179] And Jesus is ready to give His life—to lay it down in the line of duty. But He must also know that His disciples are ready for Him to lay down His life. His disciples must be ready and willing and able to carry on their part of this fight—both this first draft of eleven—and the countless recruits who will follow them. His sacrifice—however successful—will be pointless without theirs in the mopping up exercises that will follow upon His great victory.

৵◌৻

And so Jesus prays. He acknowledges to God that God sent Him into the world—into the cosmic conflict—into the war between God and the world of wayward humanity. And He

---

175 Hebrews 5:8-9.
176 Mark 13:9.
177 John 3:16.
178 John 12:27.
179 Matthew 16:21.

confirms to God that He has sent His troops to carry on the fight. They—we—have His marching orders: "Into the world."[180]

It is not a defensive strategy. God chose to invade this world—His own territory—because it had been occupied by a hostile force. This divine invasion was the only way to win back what rightfully belonged to God. As Jesus told His disciples in the Gospel of Matthew after they identified Him as Christ and Son of God, "Not even the power of death will be able to stop the attack we're going to launch against it."[181]

God, in the Person of Jesus Christ, was invading a world in determined rebellion—for the purpose of winning it back.[182] But His weapons were not to be those of His enemies. It would serve no purpose to fight the world's evil with evil.[183] God would, instead, win the world with the superior armament of sacrificial love and spiritual truth.[184]

Victory lay not in taking the lives of His enemies, but in giving His own for them. And to wield this divine weapon successfully, God's chosen Champion must be willing not merely to accept the mission—to pay the price He will have to pay in the cause of victory. He must be consecrated—sanctified—morally and spiritually worthy to represent God in this battle.[185]

And so Jesus confirms in prayer to God the Father and before His disciples that He has sanctified Himself. Through complete and willing obedience to the orders of the Father—through absolute identification with the mission God intends to accomplish—Jesus has set Himself apart.

Jesus has made Himself worthy to fight the ultimate battle for God—worthy to fight the enemies of God—natural and supernatural—and able to win the essential and glorious victory.

---

[180] Matthew 28:19-20.
[181] Matthew 16:18.
[182] Romans 5:8.
[183] Romans 12:21.
[184] Ephesians 5:2; 1 John 4:10.
[185] Hebrews 9:11-15.

And as they sit beneath the sound of the prayer of Jesus their Leader, His men the disciples learn that they have been consecrated, too. The warrior Leader not only fights the enemy bravely and wisely and successfully, He enables His followers to do the same.[186] Without Him—without the miraculous change He has brought about in them—these men of Jesus, and of God, could accomplish nothing[187]—they would always be defeated.

Jesus will send them—and us—into the world to do battle for God. Jesus sanctified them—and us—so that they and we are morally and spiritually worthy to undertake the quest our Leader sets before us. And knowing that the battles with the world lie before Him and before all those who choose to enlist in His service, Jesus prays.

He prays that we will be victorious in battle, not that we will escape it. He prays for our protection—in conflict with the world—not from it. He prays that we, having abandoned our place in the ranks of the rebellious world, will be unified and joyful in the performance of our duties in the service of our God.

He prays for the success of our mission, which is not to destroy those who belong to the world, but to recruit them—to call them out of "the world" and into the ranks of the redeemed—the sanctified—those sent by Jesus to do battle for the eternal soul of every person who is still in the world—still part of the rebellion against God. After all, the 11 men who heard this prayer spoken by Jesus Himself were originally enemies of God, until Jesus called them to come across the spiritual "no man's land" and they came.

And so were all of us, enemies of God, until we followed their example in response to the consecrated call from some spiritual foot soldier like those who pierced our defenses with the truth of God in Jesus Christ.

ॐ

---

186 John 14:12.
187 John 15:5.

And now, we are the ones Jesus prays for as His own elite force, soldiers of God but enemies of the world because of our loyalty to Him, fighting to reduce the ranks of the enemy by attacking their entrenched positions with a firepower of words—the powerful, life-transforming words of the gospel.[188]

Jesus prays and goes off to do battle—to give His "last full measure of devotion"[189]—His last living breath—so that, by the grace and will of God, those who kill Him might live.

And God His Heavenly Father hears the prayer of His Son, Jesus, for His followers. And God answers that prayer. The spiritually sanctified followers of Jesus will discover boldness[190] when they realize that Jesus has won His battle with the world and its leader. They will find themselves emboldened by the courage of their Leader and, in His Spirit, they go off to do battle—to contend, as He commanded, with the world.

And now we are His disciples, His force in the world today—in the world, but not of it. Jesus has sent us to fulfill God's mission. He has sanctified us through His sacrifice in the great and glorious Battle of the Cross. The world is still warring against the God Who made it and loves it still. And Jesus is still praying for His disciples that His example will guide and inspire us to advance into the world to take up the battle with the world—the world of people in rebellion against God—the world of which we are no longer a part.

Listen!

He's praying for you.

৯৽৻৩

---

[188] Hebrews 4:12.
[189] See *The Gettysburg Address*, November 16, 1863.
[190] Acts 4:13, 31.

24.

When Jesus Prayed for You

John 17:20-26 NRSV

[Jesus prayed:]

20 "I ask not only on behalf of these, but also on behalf of those who will believe in me through their word, 21 that they may all be one. As you, Father, are in me and I am in you, may they also be in us, so that the world may believe that you have sent me. 22 The glory that you have given me I have given them, so that they may be one, as we are one, 23 I in them and you in me, that they may become completely one, so that the world may know that you have sent me and have loved them even as you have loved me. 24 Father, I desire that those also, whom you have given me, may be with me where I am, to see my glory, which you have given me because you loved me before the foundation of the world.

25 "Righteous Father, the world does not know you, but I know you; and these know that you have sent me. 26 I made your name known to them, and I will make it known, so that the love with which you have loved me may be in them, and I in them."

༚᯲

On the back of the pew in front of you, there are hymnals and Bibles. There are also informational brochures and little white prayer cards. If you write down a request on one of those cards and drop it in one of the boxes as you leave, godly people will come every day to our Prayer Room and pray for you. If you come to our Healing Service each month, a pastor will serve you communion and pray for you. And, according to the Gospel passage we heard earlier, if you are a Christian—a believer—Jesus Himself has already prayed for you.

On the night that He was betrayed,[191] with a Lord's Supper to institute[192] and feet to wash,[193] with a betrayer to confront,[194] and bewildered disciples to prepare for His imminent crucifixion, death and burial,[195] Jesus also took time to pray—for you.

"I do not pray for these only," He said (meaning Peter, James and John and the others huddled anxiously around Him in that borrowed upper room), *"but also for those who will believe in me through their word."* And that, my Christian friend, means *you*.

And it could mean you, my *non*-Christian friend, if you come someday to believe that Jesus is Lord.

It's like listening to Jesus pray about all the great things He has to pray about—which is impressive enough—and then peeking over His shoulder at His prayer list and seeing your own name on it.

"I pray for those who will become Christians." And with that prayer, Jesus reaches forward through the centuries—and points to you—touches you. He reaches out to you and draws you back into that upper room with Him.

There's a little chorus that goes, "Lord, listen to your children praying."[196] It's in our hymnal. Today, we need to turn the words around: "Children, listen to your Lord praying." Listen to your Lord praying for you, and listen to *what* He's praying for you: *"I pray for those who will believe in Me…that they may **all** be one…."*

---

191 2 Corinthians 11:23.
192 2 Corinthians 11:25.
193 John 13:1-12.
194 Matthew 26:21-23.
195 John 13:31—16:33.
196 Ken Medema, "Lord, Listen to Your Children Praying, 1970.

When Jesus prayed for you, He did not ask the heavenly Father for your prosperity or the preservation of your freedoms. He did not even ask for deep religious commitment on your part or spectacular spiritual growth. Jesus asked God for your unity with other believers—*all* other believers: *"that they may **all** be one...."* Unity with other believers is what Jesus wanted (and still wants) most for you. That's what He asked God to give you.

Now you may have wished that Jesus had prayed for a higher return on your investments or a lower handicap, but unity with other Christians is what the Lord Who loves You and died for you asked God the Father for in His prayer for you. And lest there be any confusion, the kind of unity Jesus is praying for is the kind of unity that exists between Him and His Heavenly Father.[197]

In fact, Jesus prayed not just that you would be unified with other Christians the way He and the Father are unified; Jesus prayed to the Father that you would be unified with other Christians as a *part* of that divine and inseparable unity: *"As You, Father, are in Me and I am in You, may they also be in us..."*

You want to see unity?

Every thought Jesus had, God the Father put there. Every emotion Jesus felt was bathed in His love for the Father and subordinated to His commitment to please Him. Every word Jesus spoke revealed the Father's will and every deed He did, whether simple or miraculous, demonstrated the heart and mind of God.[198]

❧∙❦

And what is the point of this holy unity between Himself and the Father that Jesus prayed you would be a part of (*"...may they all be one...in us, so that the world may know that you have sent me."*)?

When Jesus prayed for you, He was praying that your faith in Him would be effective, not merely in saving you from the consequences of your sin, but that it would create such a wholly

---

[197] John 10:30.
[198] John 5:19-20.

unexpected oneness with other believers that those still wound up in the world around you would wake up and wonder what was going on.

Christian love that creates this unity-among-believers that Jesus prays for is not a normal part of the human experience. It is so un-normal that it is evidence of the presence of an additional, other-than–human ingredient in the mix—something so other-than-human you could reasonably call it "divine." Jesus prays that you will be part of a unified body of believers who cause the world to scratch its collective head and ask, "How can these people be like this?"[199]

And when they get the right answer, those who do come out of the world that is opposed to God will unite with you and everybody else that Jesus prayed for.

The world as a whole remains firmly opposed to God, but who exactly makes up that world-in-opposition-to-God is always subject to change. And your unity with other believers, based in the unity of Jesus with the Father, is the change agent that makes all the difference in the world—that will cause people to believe that God sent Jesus into the world.

When Jesus prayed for you, He prayed that you would experience this unity with believers that would make the world sit up and take notice. But He prayed for more than that.

"Father," He said, *"I desire that those…whom you have given me* (that's you again) *may be with me where I am, to see my glory, which you have given me because you love me…."* Now Jesus also told the Father in this prayer that the glory the Father gave Him, He gave to the believers—believers the Father also gave Him.

This is important, so let's "unpack" it.

༚᠊ᠪ

---

[199] 1 John 3:1.

First of all, God the Father—the One Who created you—Who gave you the gift of life—gave *you* as a *gift* to Jesus His Son, the One God loves as much as it is possible for God to love. And Jesus *accepted* you *from* God the Father in the same spirit of love—and *possesses* you as an infinitely valuable gift, recognizing that *you* represent the Father's deep, deep love for Him.

Jesus prayed that God would cause you to be with Him after God had raised Him from the dead—so that you would see His glory.[200]

Don't misunderstand. This is not about Jesus wanting to show off. It's about Jesus wanting to share with you all the unspeakably wonderful things that the Father has in store for Him. It's like wanting to show someone you love a spectacular sunset or share some magnificent music or breathtaking experience—only on an inexpressibly greater scale.

Jesus wants to share with you what no human eye has seen, to show you the full extent of God's love for Him—and for you. You see, the glory the Father has given Jesus, Jesus, Who loves you the way He loves the Father, has given to you: *"The glory you have given me I have given to them,"* He said. Every inspirational experience—every blessing—every sudden awareness of the presence and power of God—is a sample of that glory Jesus has given to you, the faintest scent or shadow of what He has prayed will await you, in abundance, in His presence.

When Jesus prayed for you, He prayed for something that you may never have considered. Jesus prayed for it, and, at the same time, assumed it: that God loves you with the same love that He loves Jesus. Jesus prayed, *"so that the world may know that…you have loved them, even as you have loved me—so that the love with which you have loved me may be in them…."*

స్వ

---

[200] John 14:3.

When Jesus prayed for you, He prayed some remarkable things. The cynic would say, "Fine—if He can pull it off." Our hope depends on the Father's love—not, first of all, for us—but for the Son: Will God give Jesus what He prays for?

Our hope also depends on the Son's love—not, first of all, for us—but for the Father. Does Jesus love the heavenly Father enough to do what God wants Him to do for us?

And the good news is that the Father and the Son are One *"as you, Father, are in me and I am in you,"* according to Jesus.

And so when Jesus prayed that all His disciples, generation after generation, may be one—that you may be one—there is a very high probability, statistically, that you *will* be one with other believers.

Will God give Jesus what He prays for?

If God loves Him like a son, He will.

Does Jesus love the heavenly Father enough to do what God wants Him to do for us?

Jesus will give Himself up to death for us[201]—because of His love for the Father.

The Father and the Son are One, and so when Jesus prayed, *"Father, I desire…"* the Father said, "Granted!"

"Father, I desire…"

"Granted!"

"Father, I desire…"

"Granted!"

You get the picture.

৯৬

Jesus prayed for you and for me and for all those who would come to believe through the witness of the men in that room where He was praying.

---

[201] Philippians 2:8.

Jesus assumed the success of their witness—that there would be future generations of believers. His confidence was not based on the courage or loyalty of the disciples; they would scatter within hours,[202] leaving Jesus to His fate—or His divine destiny.

His confidence was not in the ones He prayed *for*, but in the love and power and faithfulness of the One He prayed *to*. And because of His faith in the Heavenly Father to Whom He prayed, Jesus could pray with all confidence for you—could and did. And when Jesus prayed for you, the Father said, "Granted!"

"Unity, Father?"

"Granted, My Son!"

"Glory, Father?"

"Granted, My Son!"

"Love, Father?"

"Granted, for Jesus' sake, Amen!"

తింక

---

[202] Matthew 26:56.

John 18:28-37 ESV

[28] Then they led Jesus from the house of Caiaphas to the governor's headquarters. It was early morning. They themselves did not enter the governor's headquarters, so that they would not be defiled, but could eat the Passover. [29] So Pilate went outside to them and said, "What accusation do you bring against this man?" [30] They answered him, "If this man were not doing evil, we would not have delivered him over to you." [31] Pilate said to them, "Take him yourselves and judge him by your own law." The Jews said to him, "It is not lawful for us to put anyone to death." [32] This was to fulfill the word that Jesus had spoken to show by what kind of death he was going to die.

[33] So Pilate entered his headquarters again and called Jesus and said to him, "Are you the King of the Jews?" [34] Jesus answered, "Do you say this of your own accord, or did others say it to you about me?" [35] Pilate answered, "Am I a Jew? Your own nation and the chief priests have delivered you over to me. What have you done?" [36] Jesus answered, "My kingdom is not of this world. If my kingdom were of this world, my servants would have been fighting, that I might not be delivered over to the Jews. But my kingdom is not from the world." [37] Then Pilate said to him, "So you are a king?" Jesus answered, "You say that I am a king. For this purpose I was born and for this purpose I have come into the world—to bear witness to the truth. Everyone who is of the truth listens to my voice."

و<

25.

For This Reason

John 18:28-37 ESV

Why were you born?

You know when, of course. And where. You almost certainly know to whom you were born. You may even know something about how you were born, especially if there were interesting or unusual circumstances involved.

But do you know *why* you were born—why you, specifically, are here, alive, on this earth? Most people don't know why. It isn't obvious, even if you have lived a long, long time.

Life is a mystery, and no life is more mysterious than your own.

Some people ignore the mystery of life—or appear to. They get up in the morning and go about their business—whatever it is—until the day is over, when they lie down to sleep, only to repeat the process the next day and every day until one day there are no more days.

Other people want to know why they were born, even if they don't know that's what they want. They work on the mystery, trying to solve it, consciously, by the application of reason, or unconsciously, by experimentation, trying first one thing and then another to find the meaning of life—the "why."

But even those who think they have it figured out—who think they know why they are here—are often wrong, and always wrong if they think the reason for their being here has to do with what they want or like to do.

The one thing that is not a mystery is that none of us are here for ourselves. It's not about you. Nor—sadly—is it about me, either.

The mystery remains—for us.

৯১৬৩

But not for Jesus.

At the dawn of a new day—a day without the benefit of a good night's sleep—or any sleep, for that matter—Jesus—bound like a common and already convicted criminal—has been brought before a man who has himself been tied in knots, not by the question of why Jesus was born—but of why Jesus should die.

The man asking Jesus questions is the Roman prefect, or governor, of the province of Judea, a former soldier and minor nobleman named Pontius Pilate. And the first question he puts to Jesus is this, *"Are you the King of the Jews?"* "Who are You?"

Of course, Pilate knows there is no "King of the Jews." That's why Pilate has been appointed by his boss in Rome to rule Judea. The Romans got rid of the Jewish king.

But if Jesus thinks that's Who He is—and more importantly, if enough Judeans become convinced that's Who Jesus is, Pilate has a problem. The Judeans in attendance outside will reassure Pilate later in the morning that they *"have no king but Caesar,"* but Jesus isn't so forthcoming—or concerned, apparently—about Who He is.

"Are You the King of the Jews?!"

"Do you think so? Did they tell you I am?"

And all of a sudden, Pilate's face turns as red as the trim on his robes. "*I* ask the questions here! *I'm* the one doing the interrogating

172

and the judging!"—which is certainly the way it looks, on the surface, anyway, whatever the ultimate truth turns out to be.

"Your own leaders have brought You here and demanded I kill You! *What have you done?*" So now the question goes from "Who?" to "What?" And Jesus doesn't answer that question, either.

Remember when John the Baptist was in prison and sent people to Jesus to ask the "Who?" question: *"Are you the one who is to come, or shall we look for another?"* [203] Jesus answered John's "Who" question with a "what" answer: "Tell John *what* I'm *doing*—healing the sick, raising the dead, preaching good news to the poor and such."[204]

But the Roman governor is not God's forerunner. And so the answer Pilate gets from Jesus to the "what" question is an answer, of sorts, that goes back to the "who" question, and ends up with the deeper and far more remarkable "why." *"My kingdom is not of this world…. My kingdom is not from the world."*

"'*My kingdom*….?!' Okay, so You *are* a king—of some kind. Now we're getting somewhere!"

"No," Jesus corrects Pilate, "*You* say I am a king. What *I* am saying is that *why* I am here—*why* I was born into this world—is more important than the labels you or my enemies—or even my friends—slap on Me. When you understand *why* I am here, the mystery of Who I am and the matter of what I am doing will be resolved."

"For this purpose I was born and for this purpose I have come into the world—to bear witness to the truth."

ॐ◌ॐ

But wait a minute! Didn't Jesus say somewhere else that He came *"to seek and to save the lost"*[205]—to call *"sinners to repentance"*? [206]

---

[203] Matthew 11:2-3, ESV.
[204] Matthew 11:4-5.
[205] Luke 19:10, RSV.
[206] Luke 5:32, RSV.

Didn't He tell His disciples He came *"to give his life as a ransom for many"*?[207]

Yes, but all that—on a deeper level—is bearing witness to the ultimate Truth behind all reality. That Jesus would appear on this earth, saying what He said and doing what He did—being Who He was—is testimony to the greatest Truth of all.

The reason Jesus was born was to show the world that there is a God—that this God loves the world and everybody in it—that this God's love for the world and everybody in it is so great that He is *willing* to do whatever it takes to fix everything that is wrong with this world and everything that is wrong with every person in it—that this God's power is so great that He is *able* to do everything it takes to fix everything that is wrong with everything and everybody.[208]

The reason Jesus was born was not merely that God—*in* Jesus, *through* Jesus—would do everything it took to fix everything that was wrong, but that Jesus would ensure that everybody would *know* that God could do, and would do, and did do everything it took to fix everything that was wrong with everything and everybody.[209]

Jesus was born to bear witness to this greatest of all truths—by doing what He did and being Who He was—because if you know the truth—this ultimate Truth of God—this truth will set you free[210]—which is what God wants most of all for all of us: that we be free from everything that's wrong with us and the world—and that we know we are, so that we truly will be free![211] That's how much this God loves this world and everybody in it.

And that's why Jesus came into this world and why He's standing face to face with this fellow Pilate who thinks he's in

---

[207] Mark 10:45, RSV.
[208] John 3:16.
[209] John 10:25.
[210] John 8:31-32.
[211] Romans 8:2, 21.

charge of the proceedings that will send Jesus to the Cross where Jesus will fulfill God's purpose for sending Jesus into this world.

Why Jesus came into this world is no secret. Jesus bore witness to the reason, and His followers have borne witness with Him for two thousand years. And in the process of bearing witness to the great Truth of God in Jesus Christ, we have borne witness to what He did and Who He was. We bear witness now to what He is doing still in our lives, and to Who He is now, in ongoing relationship with us. Jesus knew why He was born into this world, and you who have heard and believed the truth of God to which Jesus bore witness know why, too.

❧

But does that translate into knowing why *you* were born, which was the original question posed this morning? And the answer to that question is, "Not really. Not exactly."

The reason Jesus was born is unique. He alone was sent by God to this earth to be *"the lamb of God who takes away the sins of the world."*[212] Only Jesus could bear witness to the Truth of God while *being* the Truth of God. You were not born for the same reason Jesus was born.

But if the reason for the birth of Jesus is to reveal the ultimate Truth, then the reason you were born must relate to that Truth. The reason you were born—the reason you are here—the purpose for your life has nothing to do with any purpose you have chosen or will chose for your life.

You exist for a divine purpose. And that purpose is waiting to be discovered and embraced in every circumstance in your life—in every difficulty—and every blessing.

God's purpose for giving you life may be obvious. Probably—usually—it will not be. But even when God's purpose for you

---

[212] John 1:29.

175

seems opaque—hidden—indiscernible in the chaos and confusion of life—it is there.

So let us probe a little deeper. There are some general, traditional answers to the question. One of the most famous is "to glorify God, and...enjoy Him forever."[213] Another is "to show forth His goodness and...share...His everlasting happiness in heaven."[214]

It is not unreasonable that God's purpose in giving you life would be, at least in part, so that you could join Jesus in bearing witness to the great truth of God from which you have benefited so greatly.[215] But deeper even than that may be God's desire to have you, specifically, exist so that His immeasurable love for you may be directed toward you—poured out upon you—just as He intended for you from before the beginning of time.[216]

If that's why you were born, then any purpose you make your "life purpose" that interferes with that purpose of God will run afoul of God and make a "hash" of the life that He conceived by divine design and brought into being by amazing grace and power, for Himself and for you.[217]

It's enough to make you pity poor Pilate, dressed up in his fancy Roman robes, but stripped bare inside by Jesus Who told him about a truth—the Truth—that Pilate was unwilling to accept.

Why were you born? Why are you here in "the here and now."

Jesus knew why He was born. He can probably help you a lot with your version of the question.

෨෬

---

[213] From *The Westminster Shorter Catechism*, 1647.
[214] From *The Baltimore Catechism*, 1885.
[215] 2 Corinthians 4:1-6.
[216] Psalm 139:13-16.
[217] Luke 14:25-33.

John 21:1-14 ESV

¹*After this Jesus revealed himself again to the disciples by the Sea of Tiberias, and he revealed himself in this way.* ²*Simon Peter, Thomas (called the Twin), Nathanael of Cana in Galilee, the sons of Zebedee, and two others of his disciples were together.* ³*Simon Peter said to them, "I am going fishing." They said to him, "We will go with you." They went out and got into the boat, but that night they caught nothing.*

⁴*Just as day was breaking, Jesus stood on the shore; yet the disciples did not know that it was Jesus.* ⁵*Jesus said to them, "Children, do you have any fish?" They answered him, "No."* ⁶*He said to them, "Cast the net on the right side of the boat, and you will find some." So they cast it, and now they were not able to haul it in, because of the quantity of fish.* ⁷*That disciple whom Jesus loved therefore said to Peter, "It is the Lord!" When Simon Peter heard that it was the Lord, he put on his outer garment, for he was stripped for work, and threw himself into the sea.* ⁸*The other disciples came in the boat, dragging the net full of fish, for they were not far from the land, but about a hundred yards off.*

⁹*When they got out on land, they saw a charcoal fire in place, with fish laid out on it, and bread.* ¹⁰*Jesus said to them, "Bring some of the fish that you have just caught."* ¹¹*So Simon Peter went aboard and hauled the net ashore, full of large fish, 153 of them. And although there were so many, the net was not torn.* ¹²*Jesus said to them, "Come and have breakfast." Now none of the disciples dared ask him, "Who are you?" They knew it was the Lord.* ¹³*Jesus came and took the bread and gave it to them, and so with the fish.* ¹⁴*This was now the third time that Jesus was revealed to the disciples after he was raised from the dead.*

৯৩

26.

Daybreak

John 21:1-14 ESV

Resurrection. Revelation. Recognition.

That's what this story in the Gospel of John is all about. God had raised Jesus from the dead. The resurrected Jesus reveals Himself to His disciples. And, somewhere in the process, His disciples recognize Jesus, though they didn't at first.

This is a story, not in the sense that they made it up, but in the sense that a story is when somebody tells you what happened. Some things just "are," but most things "happen." They "weren't," and then they "are." I could tell you the story of how I became a minister, or how I met my wife. You could tell me the story of how you survived the war, or how you raised your kids, or how both happen to be the same story. We tell stories to show how things happened. And so does the Bible.

This story in the Gospel of John is told as a *symbolic* story. That means it has more meaning that just what happened in the story. The story itself is true, and then there's more truth besides. It was true for the people in the story, when these things happened to them. And it is, in some deeper way, true for those who read or hear the story.

It is, in some way, your story—or can be. It is the story of Resurrection, Revelation and Recognition.

The story of the Resurrection of Jesus Christ is at the heart of the story of the Bible. Every gospel tells it.[218] Every book in the New Testament assumes it. Every book in the Old Testament tells something about how God was preparing for it. The story of the Resurrection is the greatest story in the Bible—but it is not the whole story.

If the story of the Bible ends with the Resurrection of Jesus, it is still a tragedy—a heartbreaking story, every bit as much as the one about the Crucifixion of Jesus. If the Resurrection was all that happened, it might as well *not* have happened.

Two other things had to happen for the Resurrection to be part of "The Greatest Story Ever Told."[219] The resurrected Jesus had to reveal Himself to people, and those people had to recognize Who He was, and what that meant for them.

So back to the story…

❧

Jesus had been resurrected, but His disciples are acting as though nothing had happened.

They heard what Mary Magdalene had said about the empty tomb on that Sunday morning. They had gone, Peter and John anyway—if John is the unnamed "Beloved Disciple"—to see that the tomb was empty. They even went *into* the tomb.

But then, they just went home.

And now they've gone back to Galilee and they're going fishing. There's the Resurrection, and they're going fishing!

What's happening here?

The answer is: Nothing—if Resurrection isn't followed by Revelation. If Jesus doesn't reveal Himself to you, as far as you're concerned, the Resurrection never happened. What good is the

---

[218] Matthew 28:1-10; Mark 16:1-14; Luke 24:1-36; John 20:1-20.
[219] Also the title of a movie about the life, death and resurrection of Jesus, 1965.

Resurrection—to Jesus or anybody else—if Jesus is the only One Who knows about it?

But then, according to the story, the resurrected Jesus reveals Himself to His disciples.

"Just as day was breaking, Jesus stood on the shore..." True story! And more than true.

Jesus appears—reveals Himself—as day is breaking. He stands on the edge of where they had spent the night, wasting their time in darkness. Jesus reveals Himself, and they don't see Him, or recognize Him for Who He is.

Symbolism?

Deeper truth?

Let's see.

તેન્જી

Jesus comes into your life when you are wasting your life, flailing around in the world's darkness. When Jesus reveals Himself to you it is like the dawning of a bright, new day.

But wait. Even when Jesus appears, His disciples don't recognize Him.

How can that be?

Same old story: They've gotten themselves so caught up in what they're doing that they don't—can't—recognize Jesus, even when He reveals Himself to them.

Resurrection. Revelation. And still no recognition. Two-thirds of a wonderful story is still a very sad story.

So what happens now?

The Resurrected Jesus reveals Himself some more. He appears where they can see Him.

He calls out to them in their frustration and failure. He shows them how to have a better, even miraculous, result. He invites them into His presence. He provides for their deepest need and draws them into the warmth of His intimate fellowship.

And somewhere in the process of His revelation of Himself, the light comes on. One by one, they recognize the risen Lord Who has come and revealed Himself to them. The Beloved Disciple, always quicker on the uptake, figures it out for himself. Peter, first to act, first to speak, but not always first to figure things out— Peter has to be told Who it is before recognition dawns.

But the light of day and of recognition has dawned for all of them by the time they come ashore and come alive in the presence of eternal Life Itself.

When the story began, day was breaking. Jesus stood on the shore—yet the disciples did not know that it was Jesus.

And then it happened: Resurrection. Revelation. *Recognition*!

By the end of the story—this part of it, anyway: *"... none of the disciples dared ask him, 'Who are you?' They knew it was the Lord."*

And because they knew—because they recognized that mysterious Figure on the edge of their awareness as the resurrected Christ coming to them and revealing Himself to them—the Power that raised Jesus from death to life brought the dawn of a new day for them.

❦

Now, the story is a great story. Now, it has the happiest ending a story could have. And because of that, they told the story over and over again. It's been told over and over again ever since, and we tell it again today—and will keep on telling it, over and over, every chance we get.

Resurrection. Revelation. Recognition.

It is the story that is always and forever true. And it is not just a true story; it is Truth itself. It is your truth and mine.

What is our story?

Jesus died for our sins and God raised Him from the dead to live in power and glory forever. Resurrection.

And then Revelation. The resurrected Jesus has revealed Himself to every man, woman and child for whom He died—every man, woman and child who ever lived—or ever will. The resurrected Jesus revealed Himself to you.

And you recognized Him, or not, as the resurrected Jesus—the self-revealing Christ.

If you have *not* recognized Him, He will continue to reveal Himself to you—in the darkness of your life—in the frustrations of your life—in your failures. Jesus will call to you.

He will show you how to have a better, brighter life. He will invite you into His presence and provide for your deepest need in the warmth of an intimate fellowship with Him. The resurrected Jesus will continue to reveal Himself to you until you recognize Him—as your Lord.

That is the story of salvation. That is how it happened for them. That is how it happens for you.

In order not to recognize Him, you will have to go deeper and deeper into the darkness, to avoid the dawn of the new day, because He is always light. With Him there is always the dawn of a new day. Jesus is always ensuring that the story is being told in your life so that the story always has the chance to end with *His* happy ending.

But here's something more.

❧❦

Even after you have recognized the risen Christ Who revealed Himself to you in your dark night, He continues to reveal Himself to you in the light of your bright new day. And after your spiritual daybreak, recognizing Him again and again becomes easier and easier. His calls to you are clearer. His guidance is more obvious. His presence with you is more certain and His provision for you more satisfying and complete. His fellowship grows closer and sweeter.

I'm not telling you anything you don't know. This is what you, many of you, are telling me. It's *your* story. More and more, you are recognizing Jesus in the things that are happening in your life.

More and more, *your* story tells about the resurrected Jesus revealing Himself to you all over the place, turning darkness into day, disappointment into success, uncertainty into conviction, hunger into satisfaction, and sorrow into joy.

It's like you are the Beloved Disciple the Gospel talks about. Jesus reveals Himself and you "get it." You look around and see Him—recognize Him in just about everything happening in your life. And it's almost too good—too exciting—for words.

ॐ

But you have to use words—you have to *tell* your story, because there are some Simon Peters out there who can't quite make Him out unless you point Him out to them: "Look! It's the Lord!"

And then, they recognize Him for themselves: "Hey! You're right—it *is* Him!" And day breaks for them, too.

You see, the story itself is a light in the darkness for many, many people who are looking everywhere except where Jesus is revealing Himself. They don't believe there was a Resurrection. They can't conceive that a risen Jesus could reveal Himself to them—or would, if He could. They refuse to recognize Jesus, even when He's revealing Himself right before their eyes.

And so you have to keep on telling the story of what happened—what happened in the Bible—what happened in your life—and *is* happening, to you and in you and through you, because you recognized Jesus and keep on recognizing Him, because He keeps on revealing Himself, because He was resurrected and lives in light forever.

Resurrection, Revelation and Recognition: That's *my* story, and yours, and we need to be sticking to it!

ॐ

John 21:1-19 NRSV

¹ After these things Jesus showed himself again to the disciples by the Sea of Tiberias; and he showed himself in this way. ² Gathered there together were Simon Peter, Thomas called the Twin, Nathanael of Cana in Galilee, the sons of Zebedee, and two others of his disciples. ³ Simon Peter said to them, "I am going fishing." They said to him, "We will go with you." They went out and got into the boat, but that night they caught nothing.

⁴ Just after daybreak, Jesus stood on the beach; but the disciples did not know that it was Jesus. ⁵ Jesus said to them, "Children, you have no fish, have you?" They answered him, "No." ⁶ He said to them, "Cast the net to the right side of the boat, and you will find some." So they cast it, and now they were not able to haul it in because there were so many fish. ⁷ That disciple whom Jesus loved said to Peter, "It is the Lord!" When Simon Peter heard that it was the Lord, he put on some clothes, for he was naked, and jumped into the sea. ⁸ But the other disciples came in the boat, dragging the net full of fish, for they were not far from the land, only about a hundred yards off.

⁹ When they had gone ashore, they saw a charcoal fire there, with fish on it, and bread. ¹⁰ Jesus said to them, "Bring some of the fish that you have just caught." ¹¹ So Simon Peter went aboard and hauled the net ashore, full of large fish, a hundred fifty-three of them; and though there were so many, the net was not torn. ¹² Jesus said to them, "Come and have breakfast." Now none of the disciples dared to ask him, "Who are you?" because they knew it was the Lord. ¹³ Jesus came and took the bread and gave it to them, and did the same with the fish. ¹⁴ This was now the third time that Jesus appeared to the disciples after he was raised from the dead.

¹⁵ When they had finished breakfast, Jesus said to Simon Peter, "Simon son of John, do you love me more than these?" He said to him, "Yes, Lord; you know that I love you." Jesus said to him,

"Feed my lambs." ¹⁶ A second time he said to him, "Simon son of John, do you love me?" He said to him, "Yes, Lord; you know that I love you." Jesus said to him, "Tend my sheep." ¹⁷ He said to him the third time, "Simon son of John, do you love me?" Peter felt hurt because he said to him the third time, "Do you love me?" And he said to him, "Lord, you know everything;

you know that I love you." Jesus said to him, "Feed my sheep. [18] *Very truly, I tell you, when you were younger, you used to fasten your own belt and to go wherever you wished. But when you grow old, you will stretch out your hands, and someone else will fasten a belt around you and take you where you do not wish to go."* [19] *(He said this to indicate the kind of death by which he would glorify God.) After this he said to him, "Follow me."*

∾∽

27.

The Question He Keeps Asking

John 21:1-19 NRSV

It was an amazing morning, there by the Sea of Galilee. John calls it the Sea of Tiberius, but it's the same place: Simon Peter's old stomping—and fishing—grounds—the place where Jesus found him when it all began[220]—in happier days.

Peter has come back to these familiar surroundings to get away from everything that happened in Jerusalem. Jesus was crucified in Jerusalem. And He was raised from the dead there. But before all that, Peter had promised Jesus, proudly and publicly, that he would "stick" with Him—stand up for Him—no matter what.[221] And then Peter denied Jesus—three times—very publicly, if not so proudly.[222]

The pride was gone, driven out by cowardice and shame. Peter did not *betray* his Lord into the hands of His enemies, but he did desert Jesus when the dye was cast and danger loomed large.[223] And so, having failed his Lord, Peter came back home and decided to

---

[220] Mark 1:16-18.
[221] Luke 22:33.
[222] Luke 22:54-62.
[223] Matthew 26:56.

go fishing. He was going back to that *other* business—the one he had left when he took up with Jesus.

"I am going fishing," Peter said, "I'm going back to the boats and nets and the Sea of Galilee—back to the simple life I know and understand—back to work I can do without breaking my word. I am going to be a fisher of fish. Let somebody else be a 'fisher of men.'"[224]

And as you heard, Peter spent a long, dark night doing what he wanted to do. And all he had to show for it at the end of it were an empty net and a sleepless night. He didn't do so well his first night out.

But that, and everything else, is about to change.

ॐ‧ॐ

As the light of morning dawns, there is a man standing on the shore. The Man is Jesus, of course—the Risen Lord. And, although seeing Jesus *there* is better than seeing Him hanging on a cross or bundled up and buried, there is still the business of Peter's behavior "on the night our Lord was betrayed."[225]

And there is Jesus, raised from the dead and standing on the shore, waiting to ask Peter a question that will break Peter's heart to hear. Three times, Peter failed Jesus that night in Jerusalem. And now, three times, Jesus will question Peter about his love. It is a painful question for Peter to hear Jesus ask him even once.

But Jesus doesn't ask it just once. He keeps asking it, and every time He does, it hurts even more.

But the question must be asked, if Peter is to get past his failure. It must be asked, if Peter is not to be allowed to slip into a life of moral mediocrity and spiritual malaise. It must be asked, because the answer Peter will give Jesus will be the basis for the commission that Jesus intends to give Peter.

---

[224] Matthew 4:19.
[225] 1 Corinthians 11:23.

Jesus tells Peter where to fish. Jesus fixes Peter breakfast. And Jesus asks Peter, *"Do you love Me more than these?"*

What do you say when you have already failed your dearest friend? What do you say when your actions have already proven your words to be hollow?

"Simon, son of John, do you love Me more than these?"

At one time, Peter thought he did—*knew* he did. And he said so.[226]

But what can he say now?

"Yes, Lord, you know I love you."

But Jesus keeps asking the question: *"Simon, do you love me?"*

"Lord, you **know** *I love you,"* Peter pleads.

But Jesus keeps asking the question, *"Do you love me?"*

And in agony, Peter answers Jesus, *"Lord, you know everything. You know that I love you."*

And what Peter is also saying—*praying*—in his words and tone, in his eyes and his heart, is *"Please* don't ask me again!"

And Jesus relents. He will not ask Peter this question again. He will not need to. Jesus does not ask the question unless your behavior leaves the answer in doubt.

"Do you love Me? I can't tell by what you're doing."

Loving Jesus is not finally about how you feel about Him. It's about what you do because you love Him. It's about what your love for Him drives you to do—what it will not let you *not* do.

And that is why Jesus responds to each of Peter's answers with an answer of His own: *"Feed my lambs. Tend my sheep.* Follow Me. *Do you love me?* Do what I give you to do."

ও~ৎ

Jesus will not ask Peter this question again, but that does not mean that He has stopped asking it.

---

226 Matthew 26:33.

It is the question Jesus keeps asking, And not just of Peter. Of course, if the question were just for Peter, John would not have bothered to tell us about it. It is the question Jesus asked Peter, and keeps asking every disciple like Peter.

Is your story that different from Peter's? Love experienced. Power and wisdom observed. A call to service heard and accepted. Then, impulsive promises of faithfulness and, all too soon, a heartbreaking failure to keep those promises.

Have you failed your loving Lord? Have you broken your promise of loyalty in the words you have spoken or the deeds you have done—or left undone?

Even now—even to you—Jesus will come and ask the question, "Do you love Me?"

Are you ashamed of your failures—your functional denials of your brave affirmations of faith and loyalty?

"What can I tell Him after what I've done? Jesus knows me. He knows I failed Him."

Yes, and He asks you the same question He asked Peter: *"Do you love me?"*

And He will keep asking it until He gets the answer from you He got from Peter. It is an agonizing question for Jesus to put to you. You feel bad enough as it is.

ॐ•ॐ

But there's more to this question than you think. Out of the pain of the confrontation of your failure—the agonizing and unavoidable admission of weakness and fear and desertion of Christian duty—comes something you would not expect and could not imagine: redemption—and reconciliation—and restoration.

"Do you love Me?" Jesus asks you.

And when you say, "Yes, You know that I love you," you know what He's going to tell you to do: "If you love Me, feed My lambs; if you love Me, tend My sheep."

190

In other words, "If you love Me, you are qualified to do what I want you to do."

And there's more.

Jesus keeps asking the question because within the question is a great and glorious implication.

What is His message?

Jesus would not ask you if you love Him unless He—still—loves you.

"Do you love Me? I still love you. After what you did—*despite* what you did—I—still—love you."

And the love of Jesus for you is not limited to how He feels about you. The love of Jesus has always been about what He did for you—and what He *is* doing for you—and what He *will* do for you. Jesus loves you and so He feeds you and tends to you as one of His beloved sheep. And because of that, He asks you the question again: "Do you love Me?"

Jesus says, "Feed and tend My sheep—because you love Me."

And will Jesus not—also and at the same time—be feeding and tending the same sheep He commands you to feed and tend? Jesus will be doing what He does for His sheep *through* you, just as He did through Peter.

It's as though Jesus says, "Your failure to be faithful to Me called your love into question, but because you have reaffirmed your love for Me, I give you this mission."

అ•భ

It turns out that Jesus keeps asking the question, not to punish our failures as His disciples, but to redeem us from those failures and to reward our love for Him with the opportunity to demonstrate our love in ways that are important to Him.

Of course, not everyone has denied Jesus in so flagrant a way as Peter did in Jerusalem. It is much more common to just "rearrange your priorities" as Peter does in Galilee.

Peter had been completely immersed in Jesus and His work for quite a while. Now, Peter feels like it's time to focus on something else besides Jesus. When he says he's going fishing, Peter is, in essence, announcing he's "done" with "the Jesus business."

Peter thought the "Jesus-first-and-only" phase of his life was over—when, in fact, it had hardly begun.

And yet, it turned out that everything that had gone before had just been preparation.

Our Lord will keep on asking the question until He gets the answer He wants: "Do you love Me? If you love Me, feed My lambs—tend My sheep—take care of those I love."

৯৯

From the Epistle of First John

1 John 1:5–2:2 RSV

1 *⁵ This is the message we have heard from him and proclaim to you, that God is light and in him is no darkness at all. ⁶ If we say we have fellowship with him while we walk in darkness, we lie and do not live according to the truth; ⁷ but if we walk in the light, as he is in the light, we have fellowship with one another, and the blood of Jesus his Son cleanses us from all sin. ⁸ If we say we have no sin, we deceive ourselves, and the truth is not in us. ⁹ If we confess our sins, he is faithful and just, and will forgive our sins and cleanse us from all unrighteousness. ¹⁰ If we say we have not sinned, we make him a liar, and his word is not in us.*

2 *¹ My little children, I am writing this to you so that you may not sin; but if any one does sin, we have an advocate with the Father, Jesus Christ the righteous; ² and he is the expiation for our sins, and not for ours only but also for the sins of the whole world.*

☙❧

28.

What Do We Do About Sin?

1 John 1:5–2:2 RSV

There is a problem with Christianity. It was a problem for the early church and it is a problem today. The problem has to do with the nature of God and the nature of sin and the response of man who's stuck between the two.

There are several ways to approach this problem, but not all of them are acceptable to God or beneficial for us. It's important to know the implications when we choose our position on sin. First John provides us some excellent help.

The good news is that God is light, all light, total light, no darkness.

Of course, this is not "news" in the sense that it is new information. We've been told that our God is the God of light from the beginning. In fact, in the beginning, *"God said, 'Let there be light,' and there was light."*[227] God led the children of Israel out of bondage in Egypt with a pillar of fire that lit up the night and dispelled the darkness.[228] The Psalmist confessed that God was his

---

[227] Genesis 1:3, RSV.
[228] Exodus 13:21.

"light and salvation,"[229] while prophets call upon their people to *"Arise, shine, for your light has come."*[230]

And then in the New Testament, the Gospel of John introduces Jesus by saying that *"[t]he true light that enlightens every man was coming into the world.*[231] *In him was life, and the life was the light of men. The light shines in the darkness, and the darkness has not overcome it."*[232]

The light of the world is Jesus,[233] and Jesus is the Son of a God Who is all light and no darkness. This is incredible news, but it is so familiar to us by now that we easily lose track of its significance—its wonder.

But the significance is not lost on a society bound up in a world of much too much darkness and not nearly enough light. The gospel of Jesus spreads like wildfire across an earthly empire in the wake of His Resurrection, and desperate people drink in the good news—like water in the desert. It is hope. It is joy. It is life where there was none. It is incredible light: "Finally, something besides the darkness!"

Darkness is where sin is. Sin is rebellion against God, opposition to God, hostility toward all that God has done and is doing. Sin is the effort and evidence of evil, which cannot survive in the light of God's holiness. And it is sin that seduces us human beings from our rightful relationship with this God of light, and drives us out of His light and into the darkness. So there you are: trapped in the darkness, yet drawn to the light of a God in Whom there is no darkness.

And what do you do?

---

[229] Psalm 27:1.

[230] Isaiah 60:1, RSV.

[231] John 1:9, RSV.

[232] John 1:4, RSV.

[233] Philip Paul Bliss, "The Whole World was Lost in the Darkness of Sin," 1875. The last line of each verse is, "The Light of the world is Jesus."

This is an important question, because, even if you mean to do the right thing, you can still be led astray.[234] This is the problem John is trying to correct.

The problem for these folks is that they have gotten so excited about the idea of freedom from darkness that they've sort of gone overboard. They've taken the *idea* of salvation, the *idea* of the elimination of the realm of darkness, and, in their enthusiasm for the concept, they just "defined" the problem of sin away.

These people have decided that since the God of light has sent His Son to reveal this light to a world lost in darkness, it is reasonable to assume that the darkness, and the sin that infests the darkness, have been "eliminated."

Now this is a delightful thought, one of those "wouldn't it be wonderful if..." sort of things. But the truth is: It just doesn't work that way. Salvation is not a "mind game" you play with yourself. Christianity is not about *pretending* things are the way you would like them to be.

You can't just say you have fellowship with God and continue to walk in darkness. You can't just say everything is right between you and God and keep on doing all the old sinful things you used to do with all the old sinful attitudes that used to justify them. It won't work. It's a lie and you'll still be walking around in the darkness, no matter how thick your sunglasses.

John's problem children go even farther. They're saying that because of God's wonderful salvation revealed in Jesus Christ, they have moved into a state of consciousness where they don't commit sin any more.

But that's just self-deception. They're living, not in the light of God's grace and love, but in a fantasy world, and a dangerous one at that.

---

[234] Romans 7:19.

It's dangerous because the logical next step is to say that there's really no such thing as sin. God is light and there is no darkness, so sin is just an idea. No such thing as sin really exists.

But you can't make that case with scripture. In fact, God says the opposite is true,[235] so you're calling God a liar and showing that it's not God's Word you're working with when you try to make a case for the "non-existence" of sin.

There are some people today who take this approach, but my experience suggests that there are many more people who suffer from a misunderstanding of their relationship to God and sin that moves in the opposite direction. John doesn't address this approach; so let me try to outline it for you.

❧

Too many people today seem to hear about the gospel of light and the opportunity to be freed from the darkness—and choose to remain in the darkness. Rather than claim they're in the light when they are really walking in darkness, they simply believe that the light of God is for someone else. They've been in the darkness so long they refuse to be brought out. They'd like to be in the light, of course; but they just don't think it's possible—for them.

Now these are not people who say they have no sin. To the contrary, they see their lives like the Psalmist saw his when he said: *"My sin is ever before me."* [236] And they mean it: "God could never forgive my sins. And even if He could, I just know He wouldn't."

Eventually, for these people, there is no light. There is no hope of light. There is no one, they believe, who could or would set them free from their sin and overcome their darkness.

And I don't know which misunderstanding is worse.

On one side are those who don't want to—or don't think they should have to—grapple with the pain and mess of rejecting sin. God is really kind of secondary to their primary concern, which is

---

[235] Genesis 4:6-7; Luke 22:31-32.
[236] Psalm 51:3, RSV.

to celebrate their own new condition of spiritual superiority: "Because of what I know about the light, darkness just doesn't exist–for me."

On the other side are those who can't bring themselves to risk faith in a Power beyond themselves: "Suppose I put my trust in this God of light and it doesn't work. Suppose I'm still stuck in darkness and sin. I would feel worse than if I never tried at all. Because of what I know about the darkness, light just doesn't exist–for me."

But there is another approach.

৵৽৽ড়

John says: *"...if we walk in the light, as he is in the light, we have fellowship with one another, and the blood of Jesus, his Son, purifies us from all sin."*

The call to conversion is also a call to commitment. We are to walk—to order our lives—in the light of God's revelation of His nature and His will to us. We are to follow Him, in His light, and in so doing, we do have fellowship with Him—real fellowship, not imagined. And we have real fellowship with other Christians who have made the same faith commitment. And in the process, the blood of Jesus bleaches us clean of the sin that still clings to us.

Rather than denying that we are sinners—or despairing that anything can be done about our sin—John says that we should confess our sins: *"If we confess our sins, he is faithful and just and will forgive us our sins and purify us from all unrighteousness."*

Confession requires that we acknowledge that we are sinners, but it also demonstrates a confidence that something productive will be done about our sins. Genuine confession results in divine forgiveness—and that spiritual cleansing mentioned earlier.

Instead of the nonsense of saying "sin doesn't exist"—instead of the lunacy of saying *"only* sin exists"—John says that we may live in the confidence of knowing that "if anybody does sin, we have One Who speaks to the Father in our defense—Jesus Christ, the Righteous One. He is the atoning sacrifice for our sins, and not only for our, but also for the sins of the whole world."

We don't have to "pretend" ourselves into some "fantasy nirvana." Nor do we have to settle for our own private "hell-on-earth."

God is light, and His only begotten Son, Jesus Christ, is the light of the world. And that same Jesus Christ has cleansed us of the sin that drove us into the darkness. And now that we are in the light, He continues to intercede for us with God whenever our sin might be expected to interfere with our fellowship and return us to the darkness.

Because of Jesus Christ, our problem with sin is no longer sin. Sin—our sin—is now God's problem. Our problem is choosing how we respond to the Jesus Christ Who has overcome our sin.

Do we obey Him and live in the light?

Do we tell Him the truth, and receive His forgiveness?

Do we trust Him, and know that His atonement and intercession make us right with God, now and forever?

Here's a hint: The correct answer is, "Yes, we do."

Confess your sins and be forgiven.

Trust Him and know that you are right with God.

Obey Him and live—in His light—forever.

ॐ

29.

Family Resemblance

1 John 3:1-7 NRSV

¹ See what love the Father has given us, that we should be called children of God; and that is what we are. The reason the world does not know us is that it did not know him. ² Beloved, we are God's children now; what we will be has not yet been revealed. What we do know is this: when he is revealed, we will be like him, for we will see him as he is. ³ And all who have this hope in him purify themselves, just as he is pure.

⁴ Everyone who commits sin is guilty of lawlessness; sin is lawlessness. ⁵ You know that he was revealed to take away sins, and in him there is no sin. ⁶ No one who abides in him sins; no one who sins has either seen him or known him. ⁷ Little children, let no one deceive you. Everyone who does what is right is righteous, just as he is righteous.

৵৽

Have you noticed? We're seeing more and more children around the Chapel on Sunday mornings. Easter was a marvelous madhouse, but every Sunday now, our nursery and our too-few classrooms and our hallways—and our donut table—are crowded with children.

Who are these children?

One clue is family resemblance. Some look like smaller versions of other children—their brothers and sisters. Some resemble their parents, either in physical appearance, or in mannerisms or speech. They're all somebody's children, of course. The Chapel is full of somebody's children.

You and I are Somebody's children. We are God's children. John says that we are *"called the children of God; and so we are."*

It's a bold statement to suggest that any group of people could be singled out and identified as the children of God. But John is willing to make that statement—to say that Christians are the children of God—because we are called the children of God by God Himself.

And John knows that by calling us His children, God makes us His children—in fact. It is the same process by which Joseph would make Jesus *his* child and become His earthly father in Matthew, Chapter 1.[237] Joseph names the child "Jesus," as he was instructed by an angel of God to do, and in so doing, claims Jesus as his own child.

৵৽৾

In the first chapter of the Gospel of John, the process is slightly reversed: *"to all who received [Jesus], who believed in his name, he gave power to become children of God."*[238] God claimed all the disciples of Jesus as His children. God did what was necessary to make it so.

What an incredible gift! It would be like we were suddenly written into some monarch's royal lineage or put on the allowance list—and in the will—of some enormously wealthy mogul.

What does it mean to be a child of God?

It means having the same relationship with God, receiving the same love from God, enjoying the same access to God, as Jesus Himself. To make us His children is an incredible gift of love from

---

[237] Matthew 1:18-25.
[238] John 1:12, RSV.

God. That love of God is what John emphasizes when he declares our new status as children of God.

The King James Version says, *"Behold, what manner of love the Father hath bestowed upon us!"* [239] An old hymn will ask in stunned amazement: "What wondrous love is this?" [240]

God has given us the status of children—functionally *made* us His children—because His love for us is so great—so infinitely superior to our own best intention or expression of love for Him—in both quality and in quantity.

There's a lot about God and what He's doing that we can't see or understand. But you and I can certainly see this: that God loved us so much and so well that He made us His children.

৵৽

But don't expect the world to see the family resemblance anytime soon. God the Father is calling the followers of Christ His children—and the world's reaction?

"I just don't see it."

The truth is that the world doesn't know what children of God look like. Go about your business tomorrow and see if the world recognizes you for the child of God God has called you to be. Do your godly best to show off the family resemblance. The world won't notice.

But "be not dismayed" [241]—as the saying goes—the world didn't know Jesus was the Son of God, either—and Jesus was "the spitting image" of God. [242] It's like Paul said in 1 Corinthians 2: *"None of the rulers of this age understood this; for if they had, they would not have crucified the Lord of glory."* [243]

---

[239] 1 Peter 2:9, KJV.
[240] "What Wondrous Love is This," a Southern folk hymn of unknown origin.
[241] See the hymn, "God Will Take Care of You," Civilla D. Martin, 1904.
[242] 2 Corinthians 4:4; Colossians 1:15.
[243] 1 Corinthians 2:8, RSV.

Poor world—it's hard to make out a family resemblance in the darkness. The world will never see or understand what God has done in making us His children.

߷

But it's different for us. We have come out of the world's darkness and into God's light. So, behold the love of God in doing what He did for us who follow Jesus. And behold something else: we look a lot like Jesus now—according to God's Word—we who've been born from above. We look like Jesus to God.

We didn't used to, of course. But then He called us His children and enabled us to be born again in the likeness of Jesus—to take on a family resemblance.

The resemblance is there. We will recognize it. We have to take God's word for our family resemblance now, because Jesus hasn't appeared as He's going to. The resemblance will become unmistakable when He does appear.

The contrast between what we know now and what we will know—between what we can see now and what we will be able to see—defies adequate description: *"None of the rulers of this age understood this; for if they had, they would not have crucified the Lord of glory,"* Paul said. But... *"What no eye has seen, nor ear heard, nor the heart of man conceived, God has prepared for those who love him."*[244]

It's like Isaac Watts wrote in a hymn several hundred years ago:

> "High is the rank we now possess
> But higher we shall rise,
> Though what we shall hereafter be
> Is hid from mortal eyes."[245]

---

[244] 1 Corinthians 2:9, RSV.

[245] Isaac Watts was the original author of the hymn, "Behold the Amazing Gift of Love." However, his words were thoroughly reworked to produce the words now used (and quoted here). These words were approved by the Scottish Church in 1781, and have been attributed to William Cameron.

We don't know the future like we know the present, and we can't. But we've got an idea already of what the future will be like. We're going to look a lot more like Jesus when He appears. When the Lord Jesus Christ, Who is invisible to us now, becomes visible on that great and glorious and terrible day of His return—we're going to become His "spitting image." Our final and complete transformation will be possible and will happen because we will then see Jesus just as He is.

We, who will see Jesus and recognize Him when He appears, will be able to see Him because we already bear the family resemblance—we have already been made the children of God. And in seeing Jesus as He is, we will be in the position to be completely transformed into His image in a way that those in the world—who have not known Him—never, ever will. As the hymn says:

> "Our souls we know when He appears
> Shall bear His image bright
> For all His glory full disclosed
> Shall open to our sight."[246]

&

But here's another thing: The Bible says our family resemblance to Jesus can become more pronounced now if we live as Jesus lived.[247] We can look more like Jesus now—even before He appears—by purifying ourselves like He did—by living like the children of God we are.[248]

It's called "righteous living." That's what God calls it. The point is not religious mumbo-gumbo. The point is not holier-than-thou one-upmanship. The point is faith and gratitude for—and delight in—looking like the One Who has made you part of the family. Righteous living—doing what is right morally—simply

---

[246] The fourth stanza of "Behold the Amazing Gift of Love."
[247] 1 Corinthians 15:49; Philippians 3:10, 21.
[248] 1 John 3:2.

because it *is* right—is simply the way to show God gratitude for calling us—for making us—His children.

Now, let's be clear: Doing what is right is not the *cause* of our adoption as children of God;[249] we did not and could not do enough good to get God to name us His children.[250] Doing good is not the *cause* of our becoming children of God; it is, however, the *consequence*—and therefore, the *sign* of our spiritual rebirth—of our being made God's children.

In that way, we are something like Moses who went up to see God on Mount Sinai and was transformed by a supernatural encounter with God.[251] You could see the reflection of God's glory on his face—for a while. Moses had to cover his face, first because the people were so awestruck by the reflection of his encounter with God, and then later so that they would not see that the reflection faded. Paul describes the Christian version of the experience this way: *"And we all, with unveiled face, beholding the glory of the Lord [Jesus], are being changed into his likeness from one degree of glory to another."*[252]

❧

We won't always have to take it on faith,[253] this family resemblance we're assured we have. One day, we'll see for ourselves—we'll see Jesus face to face. We'll see our resemblance to Him up close and personal. One day, we'll see how much the love of God made us like Jesus—and our eternal family legacy like His. We'll see how complete the transformation has become when we see clearly what it looks like to look like Jesus and to be the glorified child of God.

---

249 Galatians 4:3-5.
250 Ephesians 2:8-9.
251 Exodus 34:27-30.
252 2 Corinthians 3:18, RSV.
253 1 Corinthians 13:12.

For now, you just have to take John's word for it—and God's. We are God's children and we resemble Jesus now and we are going to be just like Jesus when He comes back.

For now, we come out of a world that is clueless about God and His family, and gather in the Father's house to celebrate the family resemblance—in ourselves and in our Christian brothers and sisters. And just like the little ones running through the halls and raiding the donuts, all of us children of God can enjoy the fact that we bear the image of the Heavenly Father, even if we do so now only imperfectly.

God has called us His own and is even now making sure than we maintain and mature in the family resemblance, in appearance, in manner and speech. It's a grand and glorious thing for the our church to be filled with children—those who resemble the parents who brought them—and those God has called and confirmed as His children—who resemble the Son Who one day will appear, as the Father directs, to confirm His image in us.

శు⊸కి

30.

By This We Know

1 John 3:16-24 NRSV

¹⁶ We know love by this, that he laid down his life for us—and we ought to lay down our lives for one another. ¹⁷ How does God's love abide in anyone who has the world's goods and sees a brother or sister in need and yet refuses help?

¹⁸ Little children, let us love, not in word or speech, but in truth and action. ¹⁹ And by this we will know that we are from the truth and will reassure our hearts before him ²⁰ whenever our hearts condemn us; for God is greater than our hearts, and he knows everything. ²¹ Beloved, if our hearts do not condemn us, we have boldness before God; ²² and we receive from him whatever we ask, because we obey his commandments and do what pleases him.

23 And this is his commandment, that we should believe in the name of his Son Jesus Christ and love one another, just as he has commanded us. 24 All who obey his commandments abide in him, and he abides in them. And by this we know that he abides in us, by the Spirit that he has given us.

⇛⇝

How do you know?

How do you know that you're a Christian—that you're in right relationship with God? How do you know that you are off the hook for hell and on the way to heaven?

These are things you would want to have some assurance about. You would want to know you had this stuff right. So how do you know that you have the right answer about your spiritual condition?

Well, three times in the epistle reading today, John says, *"by this we know..."*

You want to know how you know?

John's gonna tell ya.

It probably won't surprise you, but you start with love. Look at the first *"by this we know"* in verse 16: *"By this we know love...."*

Love is central to the relationship of a Christian to God, but not just any kind of love. The love required of a Christian is defined for you: *"By this we know love, that he laid down his life for us."*

The Crucifixion of Jesus—or more accurately—the willingness of Jesus to be crucified—is the supreme example of love. He chose to die so that you and I would not have to die.[254] That's God's definition of love.

The self-sacrificing love of Jesus defines the love that determines our identities as Christians. But then John says we ought to love other Christians just like that.

John illustrates, not with a tale of magnificent martyrdom, but with a simple scene of compassion: taking what you have and giving it to someone who doesn't have it, because you feel toward that person the way Jesus felt toward you when He went to the Cross for you.

Feel the compassionate love for a brother in need—and act on that feeling—and you'll know that you have the love that defines a true Christian.

...which brings us to the second *"by this we know."*

"By this we'll know we're of the truth," John says in verse 19. This time, he's pointing backward, not forward. *"If you love in truth and action, rather than word or speech,"* you're in the truth—you belong to

---

[254] Romans 3:23.

God and are part of God's reality. Actively show the kind of love God shows you and you can rest assured that you are where God wants you to be in His ultimate plan for His Creation.

But if additional assurance as to your status with God is required, John says in verse 24, *"by this we know that he abides with us, by the Spirit he has given us."* Jesus told His disciples in the Gospel of John, as He was preparing to show them the ultimate demonstration of god-like love, *"I will ask the Father and he will give you another Advocate, to be with you forever. This is the Spirit of truth...you know him, because he abides with you, and he will be in you."*[255]

How do you know the most important thing you need to know—the most important thing you will ever need to know?

It starts with love as defined by God: love in compassionate action.

It continues with the truth expressed by God through Jesus Christ His Son, in the same way: through active love.

And it is sustained by the abiding Presence of the Holy Spirit, the Advocate and Comforter God has given us to assure us that He is our God and we are His children.

How do you know the things you need to know most of all?

As the old children's song affirmed, "...the Bible tells me so."[256]

Love, truth, and abiding presence—just thought you'd want to know.

৵৵

---

[255] John 14:16-17, NRSV.
[256] Anna Bartlett Warner, "Jesus Loves Me," 1859.

From the Book of Revelation

Revelation 1:4b-8 NRSV

⁴ Grace to you and peace from him who is and who was and who is to come, and from the seven spirits who are before his throne, ⁵ and from Jesus Christ, the faithful witness, the firstborn of the dead, and the ruler of the kings of the earth.

To him who loves us and freed us from our sins by his blood, ⁶ and made us to be a kingdom, priests serving his God and Father, to him be glory and dominion forever and ever. Amen.

> *⁷ Look! He is coming with the clouds;*
> *every eye will see him,*
> *even those who pierced him;*
> *and on his account*
> *all the tribes of the earth will wail.*
> *So it is to be. Amen.*

⁸ "I am the Alpha and the Omega," says the Lord God, who is and who was and who is to come, the Almighty.

శ్రీ

32.

The Ruler of the Rulers of the World

Revelation 1:4b-8 NRSV

As you probably know, the books of the Bible were written thousands of years ago in foreign languages. They were translated into English beginning hundreds of years ago, and new versions in up-to-date English are coming out all the time.

But the Book of Revelation, the last book in the Bible, has a tendency to sound like a foreign language even when you read it in English. Listen to a little bit of Revelation—as we did this morning—and you may find yourself looking around for the English subtitles, or something to help you make sense of it. The words may be English, but the message still sounds very foreign.

And that may be because this fellow John who wrote it was less interested in making sense than in making an impression. You can't really "explain" Revelation, and you're not supposed to. Revelation is to be experienced. John wants you to see what he sees—hear what he hears—feel what he feels. John means for you to experience the revelation that God gave him—the revelation of Jesus Christ.

Even that phrase—"the revelation of Jesus Christ"—is going to require a little translation, because John has packed more than one meaning into it. This is the revelation of Jesus Christ in the sense that Jesus Christ is doing the revealing—Jesus Christ is revealing to John what he and we would not otherwise know.

You cannot find out for yourself what Jesus chooses to reveal.[257] There are mysteries and secrets and amazing truths about God hidden away from humanity just as a parent will put important things out of the reach of a child who is not ready for them, but some of the things that have been hidden from us are now being revealed by Jesus Christ.[258]

Not only is Jesus Christ the agent of this revelation; He is also the subject matter. Amazing truths and mysteries about Jesus Christ will be revealed to us in this Revelation.

You thought you knew Jesus? Just you wait! There's a lot more to know about Jesus than you know—or think you *can* know. And Jesus intends to reveal secrets about Himself you could not know except that He reveal them.

And that's just as true if you've read the Book of Revelation a hundred times as it is if you've never read a word of it. The more you read the more sense it may make. But remember, it is not intended to make sense; it is intended to make a life-changing impression on you—every time—by revealing Jesus Christ to you as you experience His revelation.

We are children of our age, products of our society. We are anchored in time by our birthdays and the limits of the human lifespan. We are locked into our culture by countless sights and sounds, by thoughts and actions rewarded or punished by the swirl of life around us.

We live now. The bulletin in your hand or on the pew beside you has today's date on it.

Next Sunday—if there is a next Sunday—the bulletin will have another date. We are now. We remember some of the past. We hope for some sort of future. But we can only "be" now—for now. That's the reality we know.

---

[257] Deuteronomy 29:29.
[258] John 1:18, RSV.

And then we are confronted with a revelation. John pulls back a curtain and there is One Who (unlike us) Is and Was and Is To Come. John doesn't give His name, but he doesn't have to. You know Who it is. You know the only One it can be.

ॐ⋅ॐ

John reveals the One Who cannot *not* be. *"Grace and peace,"* John says, "from the One Who has always "been"—Who *never* was *not*—the One Who always will *be*—Who will never, ever *not* be."

Before you "were"—before anyone you know "was"—before *anybody* "was"—or any *thing* "was"—this One John is showing us, "was."

In the same way, after everything we know is gone—after everything we can imagine is gone—after everything that will ever have existed is gone—there is One Who will remain.

And if anything else or anyone else remains, it will be because this One will have chosen to cause it to be so.

You're not going to know this from reading the paper this morning—or watching TV. You won't get it from a pleasant conversation over lunch with friends or family this week. But this truth—this ultimate truth—this ultimate reality—this One Who infinitely, eternally *is*, can be revealed to you, just as He was revealed to John—and to the prophet Isaiah before him[259]—and to Moses before *him*.[260]

John pulls back the cosmic curtain on the world as we know it and reveals the God Who calls Himself, *"the Alpha and the Omega."* Alpha and Omega—the first and last letters in the Greek alphabet—the beginning and end of everything in between—and yet that does not say enough, because God never had a beginning Himself and will never have an end. But He was *our* beginning, and He can be—wants to be—our end.

Sound foreign?

---

[259] Isaiah 44:6.
[260] Exodus 3:14.

That's Revelation—but that's not all of the Revelation. Along with—and even part of—this never-beginning, never-ending God, there is a Spirit—a Holy Spirit so powerful and perfect as to seem like seven spirits[261]—positioned before the heavenly throne of this Almighty God—poised to serve the divine will. And there is Another there in this holy Godhead. There is Jesus Christ—the Revealer and the Revealed.

And to John—and so to us—Jesus reveals that He is the faithful Witness. It doesn't sound like much in English, but you need to know that the Greek word for "witness" is "martyr." Jesus was faithful unto death, faithfully revealing to this world, in His human life among us and His human death for us, that this Alpha and Omega God was also a Father Who loved us and would free us from the curse of our sins and make us His beloved children again.

☙⤙

But Jesus is more than the faithful Witness to God's heart. Jesus is also now—as a result of the Resurrection—revealed to be the Firstborn of the dead. Though He was dead, He is now alive. The Almighty Alpha and Omega God raised Him up.

Jesus is the proof and the example—the revelation—of what all those who have died—and will die—in Christ will experience.

And John sees more: Jesus, the faithful Martyr-Witness— Jesus, the first Example of our future resurrection—is also Jesus, the Ruler of the rulers of the world.

And that would have to rank right up there as a major revelation because you don't see a Cross towering above the United Nations building in New York City these days. Pictures of Jesus don't adorn the halls of government in the capitals of the world.

---

[261] Revelation 5:6, RSV.

It would seem that the rulers of the world, as a whole, are not aware that Jesus is their Sovereign. Far too many, in their policies and pronouncements, appear to "scorn [God's] Christ and assail His ways!"[262] They neither give Him the glory that is His due, nor acknowledge His rightful dominion over them.

But they will.

$\approx\!\!\sim\!\!\bullet\!\!\sim\!\!\approx$

Paul wrote to the Philippians that *"God...highly exalted [Jesus] and gave him the name that is above every name, so that at the name of Jesus every knee should bend in heaven and on earth and under the earth, and every tongue should confess that Jesus Christ is Lord...."*[263]

What John saw looked pretty much the same: "[Jesus] is coming with the clouds; every eye will see Him...and on His account all the tribes of the earth will lament."

And what else will John see?

Great white thrones—the casting down of golden crowns—"Worthy is the Lamb!" welling up in vast choruses of praise. John sees the vision Jesus reveals to him: The Witness Who was faithful to death has become the Firstborn of the dead and will be revealed as the Ruler of the world that worldly rulers would not acknowledge, but one day will.

It's a lot of revelation; it's a lot to get your mind around. You may be thinking, "That's an awful lot of "*the*-ology." Where's the "*do*-ology?" Where's the "what do I do about all this?"

The "*do*-ology" gets revealed in the next two chapters. Some are told to *"repent and do the works you did at first."* Some are told, *"Do not fear what you are about to suffer...be faithful unto death."* Others are told, *"Hold fast what you have."* Still others, *"Awake and...remember what you received and heard."* Some are directed to invest in the enduring riches of faith that only Jesus can supply.

---

262 From Harry Emerson Fosdick, "God of Grace and God of Glory, 1930, stanza 2.
263 Philippians 2:9-11, NRSV.

Two thousand years have passed and the Book of Revelation still has a foreign feel. That's because we still live in a world oblivious to that greater, ultimate reality hidden from us behind that cosmic curtain. There are mysteries—great, godly mysteries— that cannot be discovered—that can only be revealed.

This world wants explanations. The God of this world and of all Creation offers an experience—an experience of relationship with Him, the God Who is and was and is to come—a relationship mediated by and through Jesus Christ, Who is the Firstborn of the dead because He was the faithful Witness and, therefore, will be the universally acknowledged Ruler of the rulers of the world.

What do you do?

Accept the offer.

Experience His Revelation.

❧

Revelation 7:9-17 NRSV

⁹ After this I looked, and there was a great multitude that no one could count, from every nation, from all tribes and peoples and languages, standing before the throne and before the Lamb, robed in white, with palm branches in their hands. ¹⁰ They cried out in a loud voice, saying,

> *"Salvation belongs to our God*
> *who is seated on the throne,*
> *and to the Lamb!"*

¹¹ And all the angels stood around the throne and around the elders and the four living creatures, and they fell on their faces before the throne and worshiped God, ¹² singing,

> *"Amen!*
> *Blessing and glory and wisdom*
> *and thanksgiving and honor*
> *and power and might*
> *be to our God forever and ever!*
> *Amen."*

¹³ Then one of the elders addressed me, saying, "Who are these, robed in white, and where have they come from?" ¹⁴ I said to him, "Sir, you are the one that knows."

Then he said to me,

> *"These are they*
> *who have come out of the great ordeal;*
> *they have washed their robes*
> *and made them white in the blood of the Lamb.*
> *¹⁵ For this reason*
> *they are before the throne of God,*
> *and worship him day and night*
> *within his temple,*
> *and the one who is seated on the throne*
> *will shelter them.*

¹⁶ They will hunger no more,
and thirst no more;
the sun will not strike them,
nor any scorching heat;
¹⁷ for the Lamb at the center of the throne
will be their shepherd,
and he will guide them
to springs of the water of life,
and God will wipe away every tear
from their eyes."

ॐ•ॐ

32.

Looking at Your Future

Revelation 7:9-17 NRSV

Where are you looking this morning? Where is your attention focused?

Most of the time, you focus your attention on the present, the things you are dealing with now: things like the aches and pains you woke up with—or perhaps a more serious health problem you're facing.

You may be focused on some other kind of problem you have to grapple with to get through your day—financial difficulty or interpersonal conflict. You live in the present, so it's normal to be focused on the present.

But as you get older—and especially if you have experienced some great or traumatic event—you can spend more time looking back at the past. You may talk more about it; you may only think about it. Either way, you can still spend a lot of time focused on the past.

And then there's the future.

There will be plenty of speakers in a month or two focusing on the future—at graduations across the country. They'll be talking about getting out into the world to make your mark and fulfill your dreams. But you've "been there and done that." I'm talking about the future that's far beyond this world in both time and space.

That's where the book of Revelation is looking. John is focused on the throne of God and the great, countless multitude of people gathered around it. The past has been hard and the present is getting worse, so John points to their future. And he's right to do so.

Sometimes, in the midst of all the difficulties of the day, you just need to look up and ahead and fix your eyes on the prize. Sometimes, you just need to see the glory that awaits you as a believer in Jesus Christ.

Look at your future: standing with people of every nation, race and tongue from this world, there before the throne of God and before Jesus Christ, the Lamb of God, slain as the last and complete Sacrifice for your sins—standing at the heart of heaven, robed in righteousness, washed white and pure in the Blood of the Lamb, and holding the palm branches that symbolize your victory over sin through His salvation.

You know what it's like to look at an old picture and marvel at the strange, but familiar face that is yours. "Was that me? Was I ever that young—or that thin—or that good-looking—or that happy?"

It's the same thing looking at this new picture of what *will* be. "Is that really me? Am I really going to look that wonderful and feel that joyful? Am I really going to be standing right there in front of the throne of God, singing His praises?"

Yes, you are! That's your picture: white robe, palm branches, and all. That's your future.

> *"The one who is seated on the throne will shelter them.*
> *They will hunger no more, and thirst no more;*
> *the sun will not strike them nor any scorching heat;*
> *for the Lamb at the center of the throne will be their shepherd,*
> *and he will guide them to springs of the water of life,*
> *and God will wipe away every tear from their eye."*

Sometimes, an old picture can take you back—back to a time long gone. In the same way, a new picture can take you forward, forward to the future that will come—in a sense, has come—and will never go away.

๏~๏

Where are you looking this morning?

John has the picture of your future. Focus your attention there. Fix your eyes on your prize.

> *"Blessing and glory*
> *and thanksgiving and honor*
> *and power and might*
> *be to our God forever and ever!*
> *Amen."*

๏~๏

33.

Operation Overlord

Revelation 17:14 RSV

14 ...they will make war on the Lamb,
and the Lamb will conquer them,
for he is Lord of lords and King of kings,
and those with him
are called and chosen and faithful."

⋙⋘

Sixty years ago today, more than 140,000 soldiers from Canada, Great Britain and the United States fought their way ashore across the beaches of Normandy, France, in the face of incredible enemy opposition. These D-Day landings were the focus of "Operation Overlord," the Allied plan to smash through Adolph Hitler's "Fortress Europe" and liberate a continent held hostage in the darkness of a demented, demonic power.

The Normandy invasion was the greatest invasion in all of military history.[264] But it was not the greatest invasion in *human* history. That distinction belongs to a one-Man invasion in which

---

[264] Stephen E. Ambrose, *D-Day: June 6, 1944: The Climactic Battle of World War II*, New York, NY: Simon and Schuster, 1995, p. 9.

God's Messiah left His heavenly place[265] and landed in a manger in a Jewish village.[266] Enemies contested His arrival; He barely escaped Herod's assault on Bethlehem's babies.[267] Others sought to defeat Him at every turn in His adult years.[268]

There are interesting parallels between these two invasions, and considering the one may illuminate the other.

So let us consider.

In the decade before D-Day, the Nazis had gobbled up first one country and then another[269]—and no one did anything to stop them.[270] Four years before D-Day, Hitler's army rolled over every defensive force in the Netherlands, Belgium, Luxemburg, Denmark, Norway and France that did try to oppose him.[271] By then, no one was strong enough to stop him. Hitler's hold on Europe on June 6, 1940, seemed uncontestable to many, and the temptation to defer or defect to the apparent winner was, for many, an option that served their defeated (or defeatist) attitude well.[272] And so millions of people surrendered to their greatest enemy, or fled before him.

⇛⇜

But not everyone surrendered to the enemy—or to despair.[273] There were those who believed that victory was still possible[274] and

---

[265] Philippians 2:5-6.

[266] Luke 2:4-7.

[267] Matthew 2:1-12.

[268] Matthew 14:12; 16:1-4; 26:59; Mark 3:22.

[269] Austria (1938), the Sudetenland (1938), Czechoslovakia (1939).

[270] Adolph Hitler began to defy the League of Nations in 1935 by violating the Treaty of Versailles' prohibition against German rearmament. The member nations chose not to confront him.

[271] This invasion began May 10, 1940, with all the invaded countries submitting to the Germans within six weeks.

[272] See Marshall Petain in France, Vidkun Quisling in Norway, and many government officials in Great Britain.

[273] See Winston Churchill's early speeches as Prime Minister.

[274] E.g., Churchill, governments in exile, and national resistance movements.

they began to plan and prepare for the day when they would take back the land their mortal enemy had occupied.[275]

In the same way, God was not crushed at the thought of Satan's successes. God did not—does not—yield in the face of Satan's power. The story of the Bible is—from the beginning[276] and throughout[277]—the story of God's plan and preparation to confront the devil at his strongest point and defeat him[278]—to destroy his hold on every home and heart in God's Creation and drive him from the face of God's good earth.[279]

ॐॐ

In 1940, among those fleeing before Hitler's army was the British Army. Their position hopeless, they made their way to the French port of Dunkirk and waited to be rescued from the enemy they could not withstand. And (Miracle of miracles!) 338,000 of them *were* saved, plucked from Hitler's closing fist by a misfit armada of anything that would float.

Every man celebrated his deliverance, but deliverance wasn't the point. Winston Churchill reminded the people to "be very careful not to assign to this deliverance the attributes of a victory. Wars," he said, "are not won by evacuations."[280] Three hundred, thirty-eight thousand *soldiers* of the British Army were rescued from Dunkirk *in order to fight again*—to be rested and re-supplied in order to go "back into the arena."

And here is the comparison we need to apply to the spiritual warfare underway all around us today. If your image of God's plan for and activity in our world is modeled after Dunkirk, you are

---

[275] Dwight Eisenhower arrived in Great Britain on June 25, 1942, and began preparing for the cross-channel invasion.

[276] Genesis 3:15.

[277] Zechariah 3:1-2; Matthew 25:41; Luke 10:18; Romans 16:19-20.

[278] Hebrews 2:14.

[279] Revelation 20:10.

[280] These lines were part of Churchill's June 4, 1940, "We Shall Never Surrender!" Speech to the British Parliament in London, England.

mistaken. God did not send Jesus to this world just to gather us into some mighty spiritual fortress where He could defend us from Satan's assaults. He does not rescue the perishing[281] merely for the sake of rescuing them. Yes, Jesus rescues us, and delivers us and defends us.

But that is not the point.

❧

Jesus was sent on a mission to take back God's Creation. God ordered a bold and aggressive invasion, a daring offensive strategy to take back the territory that belongs to Him but is temporarily occupied by the enemy. The more appropriate image for understanding what God is up to in our world is the Normandy invasion—"Operation Overlord." It is not God's intention to avoid defeat. His intention is to ensure victory, an overwhelming, complete, and final victory.

How do we know this?

The Bible tells us so.

From one end of the New Testament to the other, the evidence is plain to see. In the midst of the amazing visions of cosmic conflict in Revelation, a central insight is revealed in Chapter 17, verse 14: *"They will make war against the Lamb, but the Lamb will overcome them because he is Lord of lords and King of kings—and with him will be his called, chosen and faithful followers."*

Now, who are "they" who will *"make war against the Lamb"*? Revelation refers to "ten kings"—historical figures who were persecuting the church in those early days. But Paul expands the list in Ephesians, when he says that the struggle *"is not against flesh and blood, but against the rulers, against the authorities, against the powers of this dark world and against the spiritual forces of evil in the heavenly realms."*[282]

---

[281] Fanny Crosby, "Rescue the Perishing," 1869.
[282] Ephesians 6:12, NIV.

In other words, Jesus Christ, the Lamb of God Who takes away the sins of the world,[283] is at war with the devil himself, and with every human and supernatural agent marching to his cadence call of sin. It's a powerful wicked army ol' Satan leads, and his target is always the Lamb and those Jesus has taken away from Satan.

"They will make war against the Lamb," it says.

But why?

৵৵

The truth is that Satan makes war against the Lamb because he doesn't have a choice. Jesus tells His disciples in Matthew, Chapter 10, *"Do not suppose that I have come to bring peace to the earth. I did not come to bring peace, but a sword."*[284] Just as Mel Gibson's William Wallace tells his *Braveheart* comrades-in-arms that he's going to pick a fight with his English enemies,[285] so God sent Jesus to this earth to "pick a fight" with the devil and take everything in God's Creation away from him.

Luke 11 says, *"When a strong man, fully armed, guards his own house, his possessions are safe. But when someone stronger attacks and overpowers him, he takes away the armor in which the man trusted and divides up the spoils."*[286] The "strong man" is Satan; the "stronger Man" Who overpowers him is Jesus. Satan *has* to make war on the Lamb in self-defense, as futile as that is, because the Lamb of God is making war on him.

And just how does the devil fight?

Well, "dirty," of course. He isn't called "the prince of lies" and "the prince of darkness" for nothing. Long before "Baghdad Bob"—long before "Tokyo Rose" and "Axis Sallie"[287]—the devil

---

[283] John 1:29.

[284] Matthew 10:34, NIV.

[285] At least that's the way Mel Gibson's character plays it in the movie, *Braveheart*, 1995.

[286] Luke 11:21-22, NIV.

[287] Wartime propagandists for Saddam Hussain's Iraq, Imperial Japan and Nazi Germany, respectively.

has been lying and deceiving, manipulating emotions and undermining morale. He tried it on Jesus in the wilderness, but it didn't work.[288] You would think by now we would be wise to his little tricks as well. Whether we are or not, the good news is that *"the Lamb will overcome them."*

ॐ

General Eisenhower sent five divisions across the English Channel on D-Day, knowing every man would suffer and many of them would die. He sent them, knowing the cost, because he also knew that the victory had to be won, even at the cost of their lives.

God sent *one* Man across the gulf that stretches between heaven and earth, knowing, too, that the One *He* sent would suffer and die. God sent His Son because He knew that the victory over sin and death had to be won, even if the price of victory was the life of Jesus, the Lamb.

Eisenhower told his army of liberation, "We will accept nothing less than full victory!"[289]

Jesus has won the full victory over our ancient enemy, and now He leads the army of those He has personally liberated as "the Great Crusade"[290] against evil advances from the decisive battle won long ago on a beachhead called Calvary, to the final surrender of all His enemies on the glorious day of His Second Coming.

You see, *"...the Lamb will overcome because he is Lord of lords and King of kings."* They called the Normandy invasion Operation Overlord. An "overlord" is defined as "a lord who is over other lords—the absolute or supreme ruler." The coming of Jesus is God's Overlord Operation.

Jesus said, *"All authority in heaven and on earth has been given to me."*

Paul said, *"God exalted him to the highest place and gave him the name that is above every name, that at the name of Jesus every knee should bow, in*

---

[288] Matthew 4:1-11.
[289] Eisenhower's message to the D-Day invaders, June 5, 1944.
[290] Ibid.

heaven and on earth and under the earth, and every tongue confess that Jesus Christ is Lord, to the glory of God the Father."

The first tongue to confess Jesus as the Christ was Peter's,[291] and Jesus responded to that confession with a subtle but profound statement about the nature of His conflict with evil and the role His followers will play in it. Jesus says, *"On this rock* (meaning Peter, or more likely, his confession and faith) *I will build my church, and the gates of Hades will not overcome it."*[292] Notice that "gates"—like the gates of Hades—are not offensive weapons, they do not launch attacks that must be fended off. The gates are defensive barriers, whose purpose is to withstand the advance of an adversary (in this case, the Church). In the case of the Church of Jesus and the gates of Hades, the gates will fail to achieve their purpose.

Jesus is on the march. God does not intend that we hunker down and wait for Him to rescue us from the overwhelming evil all around us. That's why Paul told Timothy, *"God did not give us a spirit of timidity, but a spirit of power, of love and of self-control."*[293]

God means for us to form ranks with each other and close up, following the leadership of the Christ He has sent to redeem us, boldly advancing into enemy territory, driving the devil and his forces ever before us. We are not to fear the enemy or be intimidated by the conflict God and His church are engaged in.

જ઼ૹ

The Second World War was not going to be won at Dunkirk, or in the relative safety of London subway bomb shelters or in the peaceful living rooms of America. And today, if your Christianity does not carry you into conflict, you're not doing it right.

Many of the evils God's word condemns are condoned and celebrated by the servants of Satan in our day. Nothing will ensure

---

[291] Matthew 16:16.
[292] Matthew 16:18, KJV.
[293] 2 Timothy 1:7, RSV.

that an act or statement will get swift and vicious criticism like labeling it "Christian."

To extend the analogy, it might be fair to say that we are in the midst of the enemy's great counter-attack—a spiritual Battle of the Bulge.[294] We had grown complacent in our faith in years past, leaving ourselves ill-equipped and poorly placed to cope with the unexpected assault on our moral and spiritual and intellectual positions.

To the devil and his agents who press their temporary advantage and assure us our cause is hopeless—to those in this day who demand we give up the moral and spiritual struggle and meekly submit to their godless rule—let us say what the American general commanding Bastogne said in response to the enemy's call for surrender: "Nuts!"[295] The very successes of evil in this present time will only expose God's enemies more clearly to His superior power and accelerate their eventual and ultimate destruction.

❧

But here let us also utter a word of caution: The victory won by Jesus on the Cross, and confirmed in His Resurrection, is complete and will not be overturned. However, the victory of Jesus is not license for Christians to do whatever we please. It does not free *"his called, chosen, and faithful followers"* from strict obedience to the will and word of the One Who commands us, by His sacrifice for us and His divine authority over us.

There are "rules of engagement" that we must honor in our service to Christ. Paul said, *"For though we live in the world, we do not wage war as the world does. The weapons we fight with are not the weapons of the world. On the contrary, they have divine power to demolish strongholds. We*

---

[294] World War II battle that began in December 1944, with a surprise attack by the German forces against an unprepared American army. After making rapid advances initially, the Germans were eventually stopped and driven back.
[295] Brigadier General Anthony C. McAuliffe, acting commander of the 101st Airborne Division during the Battle of the Bulge.

demolish arguments and every pretension that sets itself up against the knowledge of God, and we take captive every thought to make it obedient to Christ."[296]

We fight alongside Jesus and this band of spiritual brothers and sisters with the weapons and tactics Jesus modeled and approved for us. Nothing else is acceptable from us in this great contest with the evil one if we are to be the faithful followers of the Lamb.

"They will make war against the Lamb, but the Lamb will overcome them because he is Lord of lords and King of kings—and with him will be his called, chosen and faithful followers."

But let's give Paul the final word: *"…thanks be to God! He gives us the victory through our Lord Jesus Christ. Therefore…stand firm. Let nothing move you. Always give yourselves fully to the work of the Lord, because you know that your labor in the Lord is not in vain."*[297]

☙◦❧

---

[296] 2 Corinthians 10:3-5, NIV.
[297] 1 Corinthians 15:57-58.

34.

What's New?

Revelation 21:5 RSV

And he who sat upon the throne said, "Behold, I make all things new."
Also he said, "Write this, for these words are trustworthy and true."

৵৽৽

Today, another new year stretches out before us. Thank God for the holidays and the time to turn away from the routine of our lives to focus on the deeper things of faith and family.

But with the coming of a new year, our instincts turn from the reflection and reverence of the Christmas season to the challenges and possibilities that lie before us. We greet each new year with predictions and resolutions. We wonder what new things the new year will bring.

And since our attention is naturally drawn to the idea of new things, perhaps you will let me take advantage of that inclination—and usher you to the foot of a great white throne, a throne like no other in all the universe. There is none other like it because it is God's throne and in the 21st Chapter of Revelation, God sits on that throne and speaks these words: *"Behold, I make all things new."*

God says more than that, but that by itself is great news!

And why is it great news?

Because, in this world, there is a lot that *isn't* new, even at the beginning of a new year. That cynical fellow in the book of Ecclesiastes said, *"…there is nothing new under the sun."*[298] He lived a long time ago, and maybe he was right then. Or maybe he was just exaggerating a little to emphasize his weariness with this tired old world.

Today, it's different. Today, there are lots of new things in our world—too many to keep up with. We are bombarded with more new things than ever before, and more still are certainly on their way in this new year.

かめ

But something about the new things of this world isn't right. We see more and more new things, but they seem to lose their newness faster and faster. The newness of this world's handiwork is temporary, and its "shelf life" gets shorter all the time.

And have you noticed: The more new things the world sends your way, the older and more confused you feel? If you don't yet, you will. New things ought to make us happy. In this world, many don't. Many new things are bad, not good. Many new things hurt rather than heal. In this world, many new things make life worse, not better.

Today, we might be tempted to say, *"everything* is new under the sun,"* but all the novelties our minds can imagine—all the technologies we have harnessed in our human quests—have not changed our basic condition.

The things that most need to be made new in this world—in human lives and human community—the world cannot change. Sin and death and pain and evil and sorrow are old things, very old things. The new things of the world don't stand a chance against them.

And God says, *"I make all things new."*

---

[298] Ecclesiastes 1:9, RSV.

Yes, it's great news—if it's true.

And why wouldn't it be true?

The world can't make all things new—and subscribes to the philosophy immortalized in the old high school cheer that went, "If we can't do it, *nobody* can!" If the world can't do it, the world does not—will not—believe that it can be done at all.

It's awfully convenient to be able to define out of existence that which does not conform to your perceptions and preferences about reality. Convenient and comforting—and possibly catastrophic, if you happen to be wrong about reality.

Of course, the world's skeptical perspective is supported by the fact that it doesn't look like all things are being made new. There's an awful lot of suffering out there—and in here. There are broken promises and broken hearts and broken lives wherever there are people. No wonder the world looks at a new year and says "same old-same old."

ॐ•৯ৡ

Then again, it didn't look like the earth revolved around the sun, but we finally caught on to the truth about that. And can you see the little viruses that cause your cold every winter?

The One Who created molecules and Milky Way galaxies and everything in between says He is doing it again, only better this time. "Behold! Look here! I am making all things new."

So believe it or not—that's your option. But remember: Just because you *don't* believe it doesn't mean it's *not* true. Just because you haven't seen it, doesn't mean it's not there.

And you might want to be careful about siding with the world on this one. The Bible says that this world and everything in it will be gone someday. And this time, most of the scientists agree, at least with that much.

But the Bible goes a bit farther: Everything about this life—about your life—is going to pass away—except for what God makes new.

If the Bible is wrong and that *isn't* true, then do the best you can, as often as you can, for as long as you can, and in the end, it's still gone—all gone. Not new, not old, not anything. Gone. You, and everything about you, will be gone forever—if it isn't true.

But suppose it is true. Suppose what Revelation says really is true.

What does it mean for the God Who rules over everything that exists to say, *"Behold, I make all things new"*? Isn't this a great promise?

No, actually, it's not. This is not a promise. God does make promises—great promises—and He keeps them all. But this is not one of them. The verb is present tense, not future. Some Bibles translate it, *"I make all things new."* Others say, *"I am making..."* None say, "I will make..."

This is not a promise, but a statement of fact. This is not what God will do someday; this is what God is doing right now—right this minute.

So if it's not a promise, why does God say it? Why does God say, *"I make all things new"*?

❧

God is telling us Who He is. God is the One Who makes all things new. That's what this Creator God does. And God reveals the essence of His nature in His actions. *"In the beginning, God created the heavens and the earth."* That's what God does. That's Who He is, then and now and for all eternity.

If you prefer the other translation—*"I am making all things new"*—what you're getting is an explanation from God of what's going on—*"on earth as it is in heaven,"* if you will. "This," says God, "is what it all means. This is the reason things are happening as they are." Divine explanation—and assurance. God is at work, continuously and effectively, without pause, distraction, or interruption, making all things new.

240

So let us say, for argument's sake, that God does make all things new, and is doing so right now. What kind of "new" are we talking about?

Go to the grocery store and you'll find a lot of things that say "New!" But most of the time, it's only the package that changed; the product inside is still the same. Your television promises you "new" attractions, but it's just more of the same, only worse. Buy the newest fashions, and styles will change. Buy a new face, and it will grow old again, despite the surgeon's skill.

God's "new" is not the typical, normal "new." The Bible uses a whole different word for this "new"[299] because God's "new" is a whole different "new." God's "new" means better, unique, wonderful. That's the kind of "new" God makes. That's the kind of "new" I could get interested in.

How about you?

ঔ•ઙ

"Behold, I make all things new." If this is a true statement, then it would, by definition, include you and me.

We come under the category of "all things." So what does it mean for us that God makes—is even now making—all things new?

Let's bring the Apostle Paul into the discussion. Paul says, *"...if anyone is in Christ, he is a new creation. The old has passed away; behold, the new has come."* [300] Paul says, *"We were...buried with Christ Jesus by baptism into death, so that as Christ was raised from the dead by the glory of the Father, we too might walk in newness of life."* [301] Paul says, *"Put on the new nature, created after the likeness of God...."* [302]

---

[299] Johannes Behm, "καινος (καινα)," *Theological Dictionary of the New Testament, Volume 3,* Gerhard Kittel, ed., Geoffrey W. Bromiley, trans., Grand Rapids, MI: William B. Eerdmans Publishing Company, 1965, pp. 447-454.
[300] 2 Corinthians 5:17, ESV.
[301] Romans 6:4, RSV.
[302] Ephesians 4:24, RSV.

In the death of Jesus Christ, God has caused our old selves to pass away. In His resurrection, we are made new, if we are willing to let go of what and who we were. We are new—new to God, which is the most important reality—but new also to ourselves, and to everyone and everything that is a part of the new creation that results from God making all things new. You are authorized by God to discard all the things about your life that were part of the old and do not fit in with the new. And in their place, God puts a new heart and a new spirit. God makes you new.

But not just you. God makes all things new. In addition to making you a new creature, giving you a new life and a new heart and a new nature, God is making your relationship with Him new, now and for all eternity.

And what does that mean for everything else in life, everything else in your world? What does that mean for your life and health and work and relationships—your dreams and disappointments—your successes and your suffering?

It means none of these things are what they were. None of them are necessarily what the world assumes, and expects you to believe, them to be. Everything is different because God is doing what God does. Everything requires a new understanding and a new approach because God has changed the meaning and purpose and value of everything. Paul again, *"From now on…we regard no one from a human point of view…."*[303]

Does that mean you've got a new car coming, or a new house? I doubt it. Those things are part of what's passing away.

But what God is doing does mean that everything you do have or will get—as well as everything you will lose—this year and throughout your life on earth has a new place in your new life, for a time, until it passes away. And in that sense, even the old things in our lives are new. Like I said—like the Bible says—*"God makes all things new."*

---

[303] 2 Corinthians 5:16, RSV.

Can God make all things new?
Does God make all things new?
Is God making all things new?
Believe it or not.
It's your decision.

≈∞≈

Indices

Sermon Titles in Alphabetical Order

Sermon Titles in Alphabetical Order

Sermon Texts in Biblical Order

Sermon Texts in Lectionary Order

Related Sermons in Other Volumes

Additional Scripture Passages Referenced

Additional Scripture Passages Referenced

Additional Scripture Passages Referenced

Additional Scripture Passages Referenced

Additional Scripture Passages Referenced